Eastern Spring:
A 2nd Gen Memoir

Eastern Spring:
A 2nd Gen Memoir

Neil Kulkarni

Winchester, UK
Washington, USA

First published by Zero Books, 2012
Zero Books is an imprint of John Hunt Publishing Ltd., Laurel House, Station Approach,
Alresford, Hants, SO24 9JH, UK
office1@o-books.net
www.o-books.com

For distributor details and how to order please visit the 'Ordering' section on our website.

ISBN: 978 1 84694 955 5

A CIP catalogue record for this book is available from the British Library.

Design: Lee Nash

Printed and bound by CPI Group (UK) Ltd, Croydon, CR0 4YY
Printed in the USA by Offset Paperback Mfrs, Inc

We operate a distinctive and ethical publishing philosophy in all
areas of our business, from our global network of authors to
production and worldwide distribution.

CONTENTS

Acknowledgements

Thanks to Luke Turner and John Doran at The Quietus for suggesting I rewrite & serialise my initial version of *Eastern Spring*, a process from which this book emerged.

Everlasting thanks to my family especially Samantha, Charlotte Katy, Jake Jerome, Georgia Aurora and Sofia Maisy Shalini for putting up with this ol' duffer, my sister Meera Kulkarni whom I entirely blame for sending me this way in the first place & my mum Rhuita Shalini Kulkarni who's knowledge & generosity has always proven invaluable.

This book is dedicated to my father Madhusudan Balaji Kulkarni (1934-1998). Thanks for the tapes and everything else dad.

Marathi: *An Indo-Aryan sub-ethnic group that inhabit the Maharashtra region and state of western India. The language they speak.*

English: *The people of England, a country of the United Kingdom. The English language as spoken in England.*

When the love & emergency credit runs out, if you lie face-down long enough you can arrange the duvet, your coat, the pillow, the floor and yourself until all light is extinguished in your world, until you live in a post-stellar universe. There is no difference between opening and closing your eyes. A panorama of pitch resolute blackness. After a while the eye adjusts, the mind ticks over, you can start picking out details. The hairs on your arm, the crook of your elbow, the bony straits and ridges of your clenched hands. A little longer, a few hours, and you start existing in this dark miniature cavern, this shrouded netherworld beneath the bedding. You, foot to head, are as tall as your eyeball, in a murky expanse where your lacklustre limbs become cliff-faces, mountain ranges viewed from the salt-lake plateau of the mattress, you start to wonder what lies beyond the wrist's horizon, who sails down your muddy veins through the valley of the clasped sheet.

I saw you, traveller, exile, walking there, tiny against the vista of creases, a dot in the tear-stained egyptian-cotton scenery. You stepped from a train, strolled up a hill, over a bridge whose lozenged walls lent your breath deep tremolo. You turned a corner the shape of the moon, near where monastery orchards once lay and got to number 7 and, somehow knowing, you knocked my door. I don't get many visitors. You will be my last.

Neil Kulkarni, August 2011

Chapter I

Sunset These Are The Elements

Vultus oriens, Ecce Homo Sacer, Rodus Dactlyus Aurora I don't have long so listen now, before your house wakes and time starts stealing your future again an ancient song for a new dawn. See the sun? Feel it in your heart. Listen to *Ghan Shyam Sundara*, from the film *Amar Bhoopali*. In 51 this movie was nominated for the Grand Prix Du Cannes, one of those rare Marathi films to gain a brief international audience, but don't watch, close yr eyes and hear. Ask yourself, as Lata's voice soars, why is this poet teaching this beautiful song to a whore, one of the whores he's dedicated his life to preaching against? Why is she singing it more beautifully than he's saying it? Vasant Desai, the composer, comes from a little strip of land in the state of Maharashtra called Konkan, same place my mum sprang from, same black sands my roots got lost in a long time ago. He created the tune that made the song a nationwide hit in India, a song you have to almost have implanted in your false-memories before you can even call yourself a Maharashtrian. The words were writ by a cowherd-poet, Honaji Bala, who lived in Maharashtra between the middles of the 18th & 19th Centuries, and the movie is the story of his life. The words are simple, littered with original Sanskrit amidst the Marathi (hence the song's ease of translation into the similarly Sanskrit-derived Bengali later), and are about the morning, the sun, and what God must do today. He must, like the rest of us, pick up pots, watch the kids, and work until sunset. These are the elements the song contains but quite why it still contains me, confounds me, remains a mystery, particularly to me. This morning, like many mornings, I hold onto it to stay alive. Because like all the Marathi music that's saved my life it's about acceptance and refusal, the need for god when you know you live on a godless planet. And though it comes from a definite place, it's in the key of me, which is a twisted, in-crisis key, as willing to be destroyed in an instant as it constantly searches for immortal renewal. You can go tomorrow morning. I hope that's good for you. I hope it's good for me.

I'll keep it short, about survival now, barely controlling those dangerous whims that could become intent, like when you were stood in assembly and a school kids death was announced and you have to bite yr lip to stop laughing. There will be similar stifled giggles tomorrow when news percolates out of this critic's final demise, I have decided to make tonight my last night of stepping in between music and you. I need no stress-ball, have no happy-place to float my mind to, rather all my life I've had this little mental trick, an invisible yet realer-than-real realer-than-me ice-cold ring of steel I can conjure at my temple that makes the heat leave, a fantasy gun-barrel beaded with my own sweat that makes the mind rest, promises deliverance, a platinum doomsday slug to my super-solipsist noggin. Enquiries have been made since about the age of 15, access to an idiot-proof fire-arm secured and ready to roll whenever I want it, only inter-rupted when its owner takes a spell behind bars. He's out at the moment, said he might pop round later and so I'm inside my house, a pop fan dying and expiring as pop dies and expires, my nerve-ends fading into obsolescence. If pop is a conversation that's reached its end, and I can't talk about or live by anything else cos it made me, in order for these exit-strategies to stay a trick and a fantasy and for me to stay alive, a different conver-sation is going to have to start. I have to find a different party to vanish myself to because this one, this black and white one called Western Pop that I haven't been able to leave until now, is played out, is populated now by the kind of white folk who say 'kmt' and the kind of black folk willing to humour them. Everyone forgetting. I have many friends. None of them can help me. I have

2

some products made of plastic that have helped me in the past. None of them can help me anymore; can only make time slip by faster, when it's precisely time I'm running out of, time I need to hold on to, time I need to spend carefully. I have a memory and a sob in my heart that it creates. Only this can save me and perhaps I've been dumb to even imagine that the white or black could lend a hand - black and white folk have always hated me anyway, as any true second-generation Paki should have learned and never forgotten a long time ago. If the only thing that ever pushed me on, the pop music you made from each other, is now actually starting to drag me down into its morass of meaningless cliché and paralysing indeterminacy then I have to conscientously object to this battle now so deoderised, wax-tipped for safety, listed into listlessness. This banter is going to have to step off its cultural-tourist treadmill between uptown and downtown, between the right and wrong side of the tracks. I don't want to sulk and scowl on these stairs any more. Tonight I wanna get rid of this writer I've been because I have nothing more to say about music and a new relationship with music to forge. My life is going to have to turn around and get possessed by quiet, earthshaking voices from elsewhere, looking and leaning eastwards and listening a while, just as music itself must listen, rather than just hurriedly thieving what's useful for the old empire, saddling shards of Chinoisery and other exotica to the same old 4/4 modes of transport before militarily rolling them down the streets back home to the 'oohs; and 'ahhhs' of the easily duped and desperate.

This is what I want to suggest to you before the night's out, that we need to recalibrate our sights to find an escape from these old tactics. Sometimes, fear of the future is the greatest reason for doing anything, and fear can point the way. And racial fear, if anything, has gotten worse in my lifetime - even though I'm of a generation that isn't in the pioneer situation my parents were in, a 2nd-generation that, perhaps cos we were *more scared than them*, rejected the timidity or politeness that was their only available response to what racial hostility they encountered. Forty, and surely by now a man and a dad and a grown-up that shouldn't be scared, carry that fear in my cells, still look out for myself and see no reflection anywhere. I grew to depend on that isolation, that throne above where you think you can't be reached. Only later with the death and onset of family, the realisation that god might as well exist for those life-and-death moments, those stopped clocks where you need magic again, do I find myself a heart and a sound head at the precise moment the nation becomes demented with tearing into each other. Until then I'm a certified dipshit, maybe still am, just realise you've come to the house of one man. This is not a movement. This will not win. But I'd like to suggest to you a new way of thinking about sound, a new direction away from the diminishing dimensions of our new glass identities. You're here because no-one else is really talking. Ask people about Indian music as processed here and they'll point you towards Madlib or Timba if smart, more likely M.I.A, fkn Diplo and his Blackberry, 70s/80s garish sleeves of second-hand disco pastiche, perhaps some bhangra, the vaguely-offensive notion of 'desi-beats' and a lot of UK hip-hop if you're lucky. Too often the treatment of Asian music displays a racial awareness & sensitivity only marginally above that of an Uncle Ben's advert. Too often, if white pop has ever looked east , in a bored sahib way, it's usually about that which can be used, dear boy; what can be salvaged from Indian pop and retooled for Western consumption, so that the Beatles can be less bored, so the Pussycat Dolls can buy a new house, so that folk on the dance-floor can throw those stupid head-moves and make the snake with the praying-hands, what stray bits of camp nonsense can get a giggle or sit with a breakbeat; or handily (but with good humour and the full acquiescence of 'bollywood') reaffirm the bouffant-barneted big trousered big collared stereotypes we're comfortable with. In the case of the best Timba, RZA & Madlib, or in the heat of a DJ Nonames track for Foreign Beggars, vintage

Indian pop is treated as pure sonics, as an equal against Jamaica & Düsseldorf & New York. In mainstream pop culture though, and throughout the mainstream media, what's going on is the reassurance of another culture getting Western culture a little bit wrong, a little bit laughable, the silly smiling Western Oriental Gentleman trying to crash the party. Like the word 'Bollywood' itself, a construct that needs the West, that can only ever be seen as a 'charming' or 'colourful' attempt to replicate Western cultural invincibility, an essentially failed occasionally 'interesting attempt' that only re-emphasises the West's inherent, inherited, immortal superiority. Sure there are more opportunities than ever to 'dabble' in music from elsewhere, but I don't judge the health of a supposedly tolerant culture by how many sidebars or specialist-sections or shitty 2-page guides it gives music from elsewhere to assuage it's guilt, I judge it by what happens when genius dies. Sure everyone's equal round here. Check the obits.

At the end of January 2011, legend, alcoholic, playback singer, classical vocalist and musical titan Bhimsen Joshi died at the age of 89. He'd been making music for 78 of those years. It is some of the greatest music ever made on this planet. Answer me – had you heard of him? There's no right or wrong answer there, only an honest one, and if the answer is no it's not yourself you should be questioning but those who made you, those who are meant to keep you informed, those who decide the fit and constrictions of what you listen to and how you listen to it. And further, what music you can pass on: music, of all types, and from all places is instinctively appealing to kids, the freshness of new sounds and words they're not used to always intriguing to young minds yet to build their mind into an impregnable edifice of 'taste'. The xenophobe cultural blockade that nurtured us Brits never admitted voices from the commonwealth that weren't easily amenable to our own orthodoxies: if we'd ever been informed of the wealth of stuff we *weren't* hearing, the shape of pop would've changed from the mainly African, American & European impulses that govern most of what we hear. Pop is stuck in congestion at the moment, all is resurfacing, no new journeys are being made. Even though current technology has made more from more places more instantly accessible than ever, listeners still proceed along tired, pot-holed roads, tied-up traffic-laden routes from which pop's sat-nav won't permit detour, never admitting that the very blood and guts of music could be saved by a look east, not just for new sounds but for new ways of thinking about music, and being a musician. Musically, we're all still looking at the same old pre-47 maps, goggling at the pink bits and wondering what savagery we're gonna step into. If we're facing a future in which, in the west at least, what can be learned is under serious threat of strangulation in the name of economic purpose and vocation, then don't be fooled into thinking that a more globalized world doesn't mean you'll end up hearing the same old hierarchies. The music from elsewhere will still be processed into what they think is fathomable to you, what can be fed into the grinder to churn out more of the same old same old. You and I have been lied to because what this music, this old, old music, suggests time and time again is not how to re-fry, reheat, or reinvigorate Western models but a whole new ancient different revolutionary way of thinking about music altogether. Surely be the next step if we're going to move on from the dwindling needy dialogue of today's monochrome eclecticism, the shackles and trade between black and white. Going back not just to accumulate shit and make ourselves look cool but to find a way to fucking live again, because right now if I keep feeling things less and less at this rate, by tomorrow I'll be in a coma. Look. The window.

See the sun? Feel it in your heart.

At times, when I want to time travel I look at the sun and I pull my arm across it, left to right, because that's my earliest memory, when all was colour and shape and sound and I saw my dad's arm flashing left-to-right across my 6 month old vision, across a window in an estate in Coventry as I goggled and doubtless dribbled outwards. Every time I do this move to this day, it moves me back through time. Now that my arm is older than my dad's was when this originally happened the magic happens even quicker, the years fall away in an instant. I go left to right, like this, and see the cartoon spirals, hear the falling clocks, feel the distant light accelerated towards at a geometric rate? Vanished through the 4th dimension to my chosen glade of reverie – I use magic not because I can. But because if where you are right now is hell, and you know it's partly because you're making it so, sometimes you have to get out even if your means are suspect & stolen and your motives cowardly. Hold my hand. Come with. Fifteen thousand days ago.

Born in Walsgrave hospital 72 and back to Wood End, Coventry. Now Cov-snob shorthand for shithole, a dream estate turned desolate warren, always like much of Cov an odd combination of blue horizon far ahead and grey step right in front of you, in my big brown eyes things were simple. Green. Space. Old folks home. No memories at all bar that arm, protection, colic, chickenpox, whooping cough and a whole lot o'love. My parents have been married five years. My mother, a Chitpavan or Konkanastha (i.e. from Konkan) Brahmin from a reformist family, is the descendent of shipwrecked reanimated corpses from Greece, Iran and the Middle East who've been dragged ashore in Konkan 3000 years ago and given life by the 6th avatar of Vishnu, Parasuram. This is as good an explanation as any (and there are many explanations) for such a remarkable woman as my mum. Her family are magicians and farmers, turn out milk and hexes and she has light skin and a look that means she's been spoken to like a native everywhere from Spain to Dubai. My

7

dad's family weren't called Kulkarni until they were given clerical jobs – Kulkarni is a name given to households in which village records are kept and maintained. 'Scribe' is the closest translation of Kulkarni, 'Lord' is the closest translation of Thakur, his family's original surname. They all have a beautiful cobalt-blue ring around their black eyes, a genetic quirk I unfortunately don't inherit. He came in 1963 on a boat that stopped in Egypt and Italy with a suitcase that 50 years later is on top of my wardrobe, she came in 1967. In 1972 I am called Neil after Neil Armstrong who was landing on the moon when I should've been born, three years previously. My elder sister was born instead, but my parents keep the name and with an unoriginality I still lament (I would've much preferred 'Buzz', or of course, 'Chilli') apply it to their son when he finally turns up. The astronaut-connection pleases me now, but nothing but milk and Fab bars and toast and breaking my sisters nice things pleases me for my first two years on planet Cov. What I can't know then, and can barely understand now, is that my genes have been 5000 years in the forging. A responsibility I've been kicking against and resigning myself to ever since my my feet started touching the floor, ever since I stopped sitting at the back of the bus cos I thought it gave me a longer ride.

A Bhramin is a fire-priest, a rememberer, one of the 4 highest castes in India. A caste you can proselytize yourself into if you're canny, but a community whose millennia-long laws of clan and marriage are, to a huge extent still, a closed system. Even though those clans have long been marrying with each other, to this day marriages within the clan will be sought, & only after those avenues have been exhausted will marriage outside be even countenanced. Bhramins are taught that we were made this way, and like the Vedas which are our texts, we are without beginning or end. Genetic research from the Europeans who found us so fascinating (incl. Hitler – the swastika is a symbol I was familiar with long before I even knew about Nazism) indicates that we were actually migrants from Iran and Central Asia, who at given points between 6000 and 4000 years ago drove the native Indian population (Dravidians) towards the south. The division of labour and specialisation that was propagated in those roaming groups made Bhramins the top of the pile, given the highest reverence, expected to perform ceremonial and ritualistic duties whilst also keeping records of village life, and having the inside word from God, if God were needed as explanatory device to the masses. We bought our Vedic rituals and fire-worship south, assimilating in the gods and rituals of the indigenous population. This synthesis creates what you might call Hinduism. We called ourselves Aryans, the Sanskrit word for 'noble ones', our caste called ourselves Brahmins and saw it as our duty to hand down the ancient rituals, to also hand down the ancient taboos & strictures & freedoms. Brahmins give women a role in ritual where Hinduism does not, but those rituals have been preserved & guarded by us zealously for thousands of years, never shared. Our ritualistic root is sound, through mantra, archaic emanations that have emotional, physical and mental effects. This is not language, or communication in its usual sense, this is the recitation of sonic phonic patterns that follow elaborate rules but have no explicit meaning. Meaning is meaningless in a mantra, this is simply what is handed down, a genuine living breathing audible relic of an otherwise inaccessible, and unimaginably ancient past. The doing, the chanting of a mantra is its point.

Not language then, but perhaps music, which, like ritual doesn't need meaning to exist. Certainly, like music, a mantra (even the ones I was taught and can falteringly recite) is a sound-object, an experience that creates emotion, but it was only later in Brahmanical history, when texts and stories started getting woven around the new gods and practices we were assimilating, that we could approach anything resembling a rational system or religious 'order'. Computer analysis of Brahmin mantras shows that they are closer to birdsong – perhaps the prayers I know and keep to myself, were performed long before human language even emerged, back when sound and it's arrangement by the throat was purely a ritual matter. A good atheist should denounce it all as bunkum, but it's the link through and beyond religion to a pre-linguistic world of nature-magic that makes Brahminism, if your name and genes denote it, less easy to shake from your system than simply a book, or a figurehead or a god.

Looking at what Brahmin history we *can* legitimately retrieve it's clear we're the big baddies in Indian history, the unfairly privileged elite keeping the masses in ignorant slavery to maintain our status. In modern India we account for about 10% of the population, in some areas that drops to less than 1%. Transplant that minority overseas and you can imagine what happens – you end up with 2nd gen kids who are not only part of a minority simply by being brown in a white country, but are part of a minority within that minority, elevated by birth to a position impossible & undesirable to maintain in a country & community where thankfully you can't flex that power or assume that holy status. Amongst particularly hard-headed soft-brained Brahmins (and I'm sure, other castes) there's a current attempt to maintain an almost medieval notion of caste & marriage over here, the usual attempt to cling to a racially pure past in fear of the inevitable interracial future. Lords of nothing, aristocrats of a long-defunct empire, spiritual leaders who's spiritual home has vanished, many of us are still subliminally expected, by our parents, to somehow rise above, keep some sliver back to the ancients, even though those parents are frequently at a loss to explain Brahminism's significance, can only frame it with books and rituals and prayers you can recite but never understand. At age 13, I am initiated properly, a sacred thread wound round my skinny torso, my head shaved in a piecemeal fashion (like many ancient Hindu ceremonies enacted now, we go through the motions of symbolic importance without going the whole uncom-

fortable hog), mantras chanted & droned into hypnosis, water
and rice and coloured dyes thrown over me and smeared on me,
my dim confusion at the whole thing still to this day a fog
unbroken by reading, only occasionally cleared by music.
Looked at from the uncharitable angle of a kid trying to fit in,
Bhraminism has been a head spinning barrier to much progress,
the insertion of astrology and philosophy and witchcraft into a
kid trying to get on being a good non-believer like everyone else.
For my folks growing up it was all more woven in with day to
day reality, the way things are rather than the way things were,
although both my mum & dad's natural leftism & teenage idoli-
sation of Ghandi meant they also knew it was a way that must
end, a system they resisted and a system that is absurd. A system
increasingly taken over in modern India by more complex
lattices of local corruption, but that still endures. By the time my
dad was 6 days old in 1934 he'd had his nose & ear pierced, had
been placed, as youngest brother of 7 kids, in the line of equigen-
iture, knew the obligations of his identity whether a soldier,
student or engineer. He did all three, and most of my dad's
generation kept & carried the ghosts of that Bhramanical past
into the new cities of technologically advancing India,
occasionally high-tailed to the mountains to meditate when the
rub between their pasts and present got too confusing, wondered
how to not lose their roots whilst irresistibly losing them, a
battleground that accompanied them all the way from the
jungles of Maharashtra to the factories of old England and a
battleground us 2nd Generation Brahmins waited in the trenches
on, waiting to see how that first wave would end up.

Within the Bhramin caste, my parents come from two distinct
branches. The Chitpavan Bhramins who are my mum's clan
could've come from Turkey, Iran, might even be Jewish in origin:
they grew in prominence as the Maratha empire extended out of
Maharashtra in the 18th century, given major roles in the Maratha
confederacy by successive Peshwas (prime ministers). They are

generally mistrusted amongst other Bhramins as being too close to the dark arts of sorcery & witchcraft, a reputation that still pursues my mum's family back in India and has dragged them into court on a few occasions. My father's family are Karhade Bhramins, darker, what a Victorian anthropologist might call exquisitely featured, i.e. with a finely-filigreed pomposity I can still detect in myself but more mongrel according to legend, bought forth from the smouldering bones of a camel, relics of the Yushan empire, vice-royalty of the lost Yuezhi tribes, depending on who's taking the piss at the time (usually my mum). Marriage between different types of Bhramins was strictly forbidden for centuries, only relaxing in the 20th century as travel to the big smoke of Bombay and the dwindling of security & jobs in the rural communities that are Bhramin strongholds really sets in. Consequently I'm a mongrel like everyone else, but I'm also made of two families, Kulkarnis and Dandekars (my mum's maiden-name) whose roots were ancient and lost in the dizzying movements of people thousands of years ago. I can point to a point on the map where I'm from. I can point to points on the map where my folks are from. But where their folks came from is more complicated, becomes more mystical the closer you try and hold it. Digging as I tentatively did growing up, into my family's backgrounds I heard stories that horrified me, about Aunties married at 10, widowed at 12, spending the rest of their lives in head-shaven shame. I heard stories that entranced me, of spells, and creatures and ghosts that walk our farmlands, the dizzy dream of the palaces we could have if we ever followed ol' Enoch's advice, cashed in and returned home. We, me, my mum, my dad, my sister, were living relics, and when I look to our antiquary I feel simultaneously warmed by its age but confused by its mystical distance. We've been tutored by modernity's hype & hurry to think that if we ever hark back, it's to simpler times, easier structures, a clear sense of place and space. What actually emerges, when you turn back and prod your roots, is that they're suggestive of a time when the array of influences on your life were way more variegated than the brute simplistic confines of categories as nebulous & fashionable as ego, or your personality, or your beliefs or your income or your 'class'. And you'll never know, even if your lazy 20th century ass is properly careful about surmising anything about people who were always dirtdirtpoor and worked unimaginably hard, whether they felt freer than you'll ever be. You would have been, at various times in your ancestors' past, a magician, a mystic, an ascetic, a spreader of manure, a spouter of glossolalia, a milker of the herd, more important than a king but seeking a smallness and superfluity beyond the sub-atomic, consulted by the great, hated by the good.

My dad had 4 elder brothers, 2 elder sisters, and a little sister who also ended up in England (big up the Deo-Kulkarni Woodford Massive). Their births spanned the first 3 decades of the 20th Century. One of his elder brothers was called Shridhar. Everyone called him Abba because everyone in India has a real name and a used name and usually a birth-date that doesn't translate to our calendar (my mum came over, only knew her birthday was a certain point in April, so put down 1st April on the first form she had to fill in & of course it had to stick – me and my sister still have a chuckle about that every year). Abba was a poet and writer, a freedom fighter, teacher, Shakespeare-obsessive & had to elope with his lover to marry her because she was a Konkanastha Bhramin and he a Karhade - it's odd to think that his younger brother, my dad, would only 20 years later have an arranged marriage with a Konkanastha Brahmin, my mum, not only without the need for midnight dashes by rickshaw & boat but with the full blessing of both families, families whom increasingly through the last years of the Raj & the new years of independence, were en-masse flying their rural poverty for the hunger & heat of Mumbai. My parents grew up in changing times for India, times that perhaps changed a bit too much & too fast for some, hence India's current vacillation between benev-olent technocracy & rural-nostalgic fascism – they were part of the first generations in India to see through, with moral clarity, the absurdity and horror of the old rules and the old life, the first generation, with Nehru (another Brahmin from Kashmir) at the helm, to truly accept secularization, understand its importance in positioning India to be ready to slide into the modern world.

Being a Bhramin, particularly a Chitpavan/Konkanastha Brahmin, has frequently been at odds with that modernisation. The hard-line Bhramin Hindu-nationalists (*Hindutva*) in Nehru's party would eventually break his will to govern. Chitpavan Brahmins, a small world within a world, made up most of the Hindu-nationalist assassins of Gandhi, and innocent Chitpavan communities faced public rage that spread in a state-wide explosion of anti-Konkanastha thuggery the night after Gandhi's death. My mum remembers our banana-field burned, her father my granddad (who I met once, as a month-old baby), surveying the smouldering vista and declaring 'old people, who know us . . . did not do this" - family friends who'd left Pural, her village, for Mumbai found themselves fleeing back to seek shelter in our stables & barns, particularly those who shared a surname and family with the assassin, Nathuram Godse. Small world of agitants, extremists, intellectuals, mystics. The man who blessed Gandhi's assassins before the act was also a Maharashtra Brahmin. Like our Abba a poet, playwright, writer and scholar, like my mum a Konkanastha, like many of their generation amongst the first to demand the dismantling of the caste system - Vinayak Damodar Savakar came from just down the jungle path. He was also a terrorist, nationalist & self-avowed pragmatic realist who through his writings gave birth to the Hindutva movement currently polluting India's body-politic. Chitpavan's have a history of rabble-rousing in this regard: the British called them 'the Pune Brahmins' and singled them out as a community to be watched. In a secret letter dated 09 July 1879, the then

Governor of Bombay Province Sir Richard Temple wrote to Viceroy Lord Lytton, *"The Chitpavans imagine that some day, more or less remote, the British shall be made to retire, into that darkness where the Moguls retired. Any fine morning, an observant visitor may ride through the streets of Poona and mark the scowl with which so many persons regard this stranger"*. In his book Indian Unrest (1910), Sir Valentine Chirol wrote, *"Among Chitpavan Brahmins there has undoubtedly been preserved for the last hundred years...an unbroken tradition of hatred towards the British rule, an undying hope that it may some day be subverted and their own ascendancy restored"*. Balchandra Tilak, who Chirol famously dubbed 'Father of the Indian unrest', was a Chitpavan Brahmin and first leader of the Indian Independence league, born a year before the armed-uprising of 1857. In the mid-stages of a busy life he wrote a wonderfully suggestive book in 1903 (in the midst of his far more important nationalist, insurrectionist & terrorist activities) called The Arctic Home In The Vedas, wherein he argued that the Vedas could only have been composed in the Arctic before Aryan bards brought them south after the onset of the last ice age. Looking at my mum's features, I can almost believe it, or at least understand how Tilak might seek that explanation for his own unique, out-of-step Konkanastha skin tone. Tilak saw this as a positivist explanation for what had previously only been myth, that Chitpavan meant 'corpse saved from the funeral pyre', a reference to skin colour & their uncanny avoidance of Buddhist persecution. Likely also that Tilak believed the rumours that Chitpavans had purer Aryan blood than any other Hindus - Chitpavans have let the rumours about them grow, unconcerned, unapologetic for their slippage back into myth – in a way I see mirrors between their visible oddity in India and my self-perceived oddity here. I also see mirrors in how, in resistance to the English a hundred years ago, different Chitpavans reacted differently – some seeing the issue as one of anti-imperialism, socialism and progress beyond religion, others seeing the struggle as religious, essentially about claiming back what belongs to a people, including a chance to wipe the slate clean and create a new ethnic purity in being Indian. For all Chitpavans, struggle against the British wasn't just that of the downtrodden against a new persecuter – it carried the ferocity of the dispossessed racial aristocracy, inspired by western revolution to see their moment to return to their *proper* status. My mum remembers being told by her elderly great-aunt, for whom the Aryan past of the Chitpavan's wasn't a literary-motif or theory but a fact taught to her and her grandparents in turn: "To be reborn a human makes you special. To be reborn a Brahmin makes you even more special. To be reborn a Chitpavan Brahmin, makes you one of the most special people on earth." You can understand how Chitpavan Brahmin's have seen their destiny and India's destiny as intertwined, how passionate unhinged ambition can be accepted as an ancient trait. Despite his theories, Tilak's nationalism and demand for self-rule was always a secular vision, even if his resistance to appeasement kept him at the extreme, nationalist end of the Congress, with the kind of anti-moderates who attracted the most violent radicals. Religion mattered hugely to him, but his nemesis was the British, not the races and religions within India he saw as equally important. When, in 1908 he was arrested for sedition by the British Govt. (for supporting 2 'revolutionaries'/train-bombers' in the *Kesari* newspaper he wrote & self-published), he asked a young lawyer called Muhammed Al Jinnah to defend him. My granddad read *Kesari*, my mum remembers him spreading it out on the ground and reading it cover to cover, she also recalls him firmly rejecting the anti-Islamic filth spewed by Tilak's more extremist comrades and disciples, the intolerance that didn't reflect the open-house diversity of friends our family always had. Emerging from imprisonment Tilak was a more mellow, chastened, non-violent voice but his words had always lit fires, and it's his political disciples who take them to an extreme new frenzy. 2 years before his hiring of the future creator of Pakistan, plague had broken out in Pune, the old capital city of the Peshwas who first boosted the Chitpavan Brahmins into politics. Heavy-handedly dealt with by English civil-servant W.C.Rand's Special Plague committee & the British army, Tilak heard reports of rapes & intrusion & thuggery & theft & blasphemy, sees an opening & writes inflammatory articles in *Kesari*, citing the *Gita* & insisting *'no blame could be attached to anyone who killed an oppressor without any thought of reward'*. The next day Rand & another officer are shot and killed by the 3 Chafekar brothers, Pune-born musicians, Tilak is charged with incitement and given 18 months, the three Chafekar brothers & an accomplice are publicly hanged. Like Godse, Chafekar's a surname famililar in our home, their descendants are part of our family. The Chafekar-bros hanging is remembered as a crucial moment of tragedy & turnaround by all Maharashtrians, but Vinayak Damodar Savarkar, at the time a young man progressing past local Muslim-bashing to a more militant strain of nastiness, sees it as life-forming. When Tilak emerges from prison and adopts the slogan *"Swaraj (self-rule) is my birth-right and I shall have it"* Savakar devotes his life to explaining and bringing about *Swaraj* and sees Tilak as his guru. Savakar's *Swaraj* however, as expounded in his books, poetry, plays & political activity was a scarier kind of rule than Tilak's, more spuriously founded on his own fascistic philosophies, and insistent on Hinduism as being the key to the religious reform needed, or rather *Hindutva*, his atheistic vision of Hinduism as grisly fusion of patriotism, common blood and fatherland. Seeing any compromise with the Muslims (esp Jinnah's Muslim League') as appeasement and one-way, he rejects Islamic separatism (in 47 he issues delighted statements about the formation of Israel), and at rallies & marches spouts threatening warnings that Muslims should not expect 'special treatment' in a post-British India, could only 'expect representation in proportion to their minority status'. Savakar's militancy grows when he studies in London in the 30s, his sophisticated terrorist plans to suicide-bomb the capital of the Empire scuppered by the British government and leading to his imprisonment, then escape, then re-capture. .My granddad, and his kids, quickly spot Savakar for the lunatic he is – something made plain by his desire in WW2 to seek rapprochement with the axis powers in order to fight the British, a batshit proposal that fellow psychopath & Indian Independence leading light Subhash Chandrihsda Bose took all the way to a deal with the Japanese. Hatred of the English translated into a lot of fascist sympathy in WW2 India from both Hindu-nationalists and Muslim-separatists: to this day, accusing Savakar's ancestors in the Indian far-right of 'fascism' frequently engenders an instant retaliatory accusation of 'colonial tricks'. Even so, by 1947 Savakar's murky connection with the assassination of Gandhi made him a political outcast and a hated figure by many of my parents generation. Savarkar commits suicide by starvation in 1966 still protesting his innocence, a martyrdom that ensures his prison writings and *Hindutva* philosophy cast long shadows over modern India, shadows perhaps more damaging than those cast by Lashkar-e-Taiba, the Islamic fundamentalist group responsible for the 2008 Mumbai attacks. What Savakar says feeds directly into the workings of the *Sang Parivah* movement, the umbrella organisation whose roster of political affiliates includes the virulently Islamophobic BJP & RSS parties. Of course, Bollywood loves him, this poet who wrote his lines with thorns and stones in his cell wall – he's a 'hero' like Michael Collins, a figure whose righteous anti-Britishness masks his actual words and deeds. In 2010 a lavish labour-of-love biopic *Veer Savarkar* is made by long-time right-winger,RSS supporter, and Marathi-film legend Sudhir Phadke, a release that hips me to the fact that one of my favourite ever Marathi composers is also a wielder of the Saffron swastika, casting a new light on the beautiful Marathi songs he's filled my life with. As I find later, this taint, this fine-line between pride and dogmatism is something that many of my favourite singers & composers in Marathi song stomp over, and in doing so stomp over my love for them.

No movie was ever made about my Uncle Abba, but I'll always go for the inscription on the only photo I have of him over Savakar's bigotry any day: "I don't want to teach you to know, but to interpret . . . " . He grew up, like Tilak, like Savakar, between Brahminism's ancient roles and new political ambitions but he chose love & teaching over fear and loathing. Brahmanism, in the 20th century, meant choosing between the past and the future, for me not life or death, for those only a few decades older than me, absolutely that. The definitions of Bharat, or India, were, are, still up for grabs – but being a Brahmin (and there are Buddhist, Jain & Sikh Bhramins too), being a Hindu, isn't a choice at all, and that's why Savakar's lies permeated so deep, twisted pride so completely into chauvinism. Hinduism, even if you're a carey-sharey Hindu as I am, is nothing you can join, no matter what the Hare Krishnas or new-agers think. It's something you're born as. Taking part in Hindu ceremonies, sitting in Hindu temples, is forbidden to no-one, anyone of any faith can be part of them. But *being* a Hindu is something you don't have a choice in, something you can't just step into with the pass of a bindi on your forehead. Where Savakar saw Hinduism's history as meaning we own/deserve something, some piece of the rock, I like to think me my dad & my uncles know that the precise fact we're born Hindus means we have only one duty. To try and figure out what the hell that means. Start reading back dictionary definitions of the supposed 'beliefs' that have been foisted upon you by your Hinduism and you'll be puzzled . We believe in an afterlife? Well some of us do, some of us don't believe in life at all. We believe in God? Well, some of us did, many huge schools of Vedic thought saw no need for him. We're vegetarians? Well I'm descended from 5000 years of Bhramin stock and I'm sat in my little chair in Wood End aged 3 eating crispy bacon and waiting for Friday night's treat of Goblin burgers out of a tin. Bhramins, as peddlers of the mystic, as my uncles and father and I understand it, have always moved around, and adapted wherever they've settled, ended up having ketchup with their bhajis like all good Hindus, can't be tied to notions of nationhood without explicitly *denying* their past, not affirming it. The populations I'm talking about, especially in the context of such a vast nation as India, are tiny – Karhade Brahmins number about 60,000 in the whole world, Chitpavan just shy of 100,000. Strict introversion of those societies has kept those numbers low, my parents were of the first to freely break those bounds and marry 'outside' their Bhramin-clan, and they also were amongst the first to feel a slight shame in what they were, a distaste for the ideas of hierarchy and birthright that seemed entirely out of place in the new secular India they were growing up in. To a point, that rapid secular progression has meant the history and genealogies of these tribes has disappeared into the obscurity of local knowledge and temple-scriptures, in my mum's case a whole language has been lost, Konknii, spoken by her elders but never by her friends and containing words unheard anywhere else in India, now vanished. Such vanishings of the past, in the rush to the cities that accompanies independence bred a dangerous obscurity that breeds myth and misinterpretation. But even given that increasing obscurity, even given the perilous 20th century history of when Brahmins start historicising, it was clear, and always made clear to me, that we, esp. me and my sister, were special, came from something that though incompatible with the modern world still warranted remembrance and absorption. A Brahminism that could somehow stay, not intrude, and be a positive force. Put that mindset in a country where you're just another nigger, just another wog, just another (my personal fave) blackistani, and you're headed for trouble, if not for the outside world, then for the internal world within. Born a problem. It's taken me a long long time to realise I wouldn't, and couldn't, have it any other way.

In 76 we move to Stoke Aldermoor, Coventry. No space. Another old people's home. Still no memories bar nights of pain and illness, days of matchbox cars and pillow fights. Starting, perhaps, to realise that indoors and solitude is safety, suits me. One day, my sister thinks she's killed me but it's just one of the few, occasionally self-inflicted concussions that I chart my early childhood with. Trapped in the lift I can't understand to step back from the door and cry until I fall back. Door opens, a swimming sea of concerned faces, 90 year olds, people who remember when it was all fields and farms around the disparate villages that Coventry was. I toddle, inspected from above by people born in the previous century, people who occasionally die, bequeath their snuff tins to their cell-mates, good spreads, roll out the barrel. Wonderful people with terrifying lives and pasts of their own, themselves born in Britain's imperialist days, people who recall workhouses and orphanages, people with vintage manners not reflected out in the street, where I start to learn that dogs and other kids, don't really like me. At 3, my parents are worried that I'm deaf as I flatly refuse to speak. Speech therapist finds out that I can speak but am too shy, a problem I will later bequeath to my own kids. It's from this moment, of being played tapes in a surgery, and being asked to respond and speak that sound finally enters my memories in about 76. Through this process my parents worries are allayed. Sound, and the recordings of it, become an obsession, the sense I choose to lose myself in beyond all others. I become instinctively hungry for music, and the processes of making it happen through buttons pressed and plastic placed. Records have been given to us by friendly staff at the old-folks home and they make their way up to our little flat and onto the Dansette. I'm starting to watch way too much telly, I hear the Seekers and Charlie Drake and see the Sex Pistols on telly and Val Doonican and

Johnny Cash & it all sounds the same but it all has rhythms popping under my skin. In a few years, in our new home, me and my sister will conduct yay/nay boos and hisses to the run-down on TOTP lolling on the floor, thumbs raised or lowered like Roman emperors as each hit flashes past. I also hear orchestral music for the first time in our last year at Aldermoor thanks to a few '100 Greatest Tunes' records, and that blows my tiny mind, puts me on the 40 year chase for melody I'm still engaged in. But there's another song I hear just before we move. A song that takes me out of the here and now realities of others, and magic-carpets me back, scarily, to myself.

This song I don't see on Top Of The Pops or hear on the radio or learn at school, it's played in a quieter, sleepier moment, a moment I can neither precociously conduct with a knitting needle or dance to, a moment in which I realise that songs can make me cry and choke, that there's something inexplicable yet immensely intimate about music, even if the identity it touches on is something I have no awareness of. The song is called *Ghanu Waje* and is played to me by my dad on a Phillips EL3538 reel-to-reel tape machine. Straight away, I can tell it's not from round here, I can tell it's from another place. Later, I learn what the words mean and it's clear not just that this is music from elsewhere but that this is music created by people with different concerns than the love and romance that seems to dictate all the Western pop I hear. *"The clouds softly rumble/The wind sings a melody/the shelter/the moonlight/Champak flower & sandalwood/I have no desire without you . . ."* The song sounds soft and glowing like moonlight, like shelter, but is about looking in the mirror and not seeing yourself looking back, *"I anoint myself with sandalwood/But it burns my body/It is said the bed of flowers is soothing/but it scorches me like fire/ Oh you cuckoo birds/cease your sweet song/ When I look into a mirror/it's not my reflection I see/God has done this to me'*. The vocal swoops and melodic teasings transform God into your lover, then says there is no distinction between the lover and the loved one. It says that Krishna is you, that you can blend your blues with his reds and become one blackness. It's by Maharashtrians of a similar vintage to my parents, Hridaynath Mangeshkar and his sister Lata, a familial combination that created gold whenever it collaborated... but at age five I knew none of this. I just knew it felt funny, that this song woke and walked into new chambers of my still-growing heart, instrumentation I couldn't quite picture that pulled the brine from your eyes in pure melodic yearning and sent you on through your day levitating a few inches above the ground. A poem that's over 1000 years old. Hits you like it were writ tomorrow. With music growing in my life, but this song keeping a creepy, unwavering presence within, we move elsewhere in 78. Revolutions Per Minute, learning new things, new prone shapes to throw, new realities. Like real sadness. Like real fear.

Chapter 2

An Extreme New Form Of Englander

As ever, I don't remember the important stuff, the van, the packing, the boxes, the miracle of a garden. I just remember knowing I was somewhere tougher than before. Move to Ernsford Grange, Coventry in 78. Make friends finally, now I'm not up in the flats in an old-folks home and living in a house on a street. Catch bus to and from school with sister, latchkey kids. House down the road, 'the punk house', occasionally skinheads snarling & spitting my way, fear of fascist attack locked inside forever, chip on shoulder budding already. One close close white friend, play everywhere with him, like all my intense childhood friendships it ends in desertion and/or horror. Late 1980 he asks me out to play post-cherryade Sunday afternoon. Make it down the corner, his other friends waiting with a water bomb and a few well-placed punches and a few new words they've learned like paki and nignog and wog and blackie, words I'd heard at school behind my back but that had not yet been spat at me like this. Blub and it makes them hit harder. Teaches me something very important. 2 years later in 82, in retrospect, as a slightly hardened, ready to defend myself 10 year old still thinking about it, as I do for a while, I come to a conclusion I still haven't been able to shake. *Don't trust them to understand you, ever, there's a wall there that can never be breached, a wall that's taken too long to build, that's too important to a lot of people to ever come down.* As I eventually realise, in moments of national crisis, whether 81 or 2011, when the search for scapegoats becomes paramount, the wall will be sat on once more and you will be watched from it, the issue that you are batted around again with that familiar mix of patrician disappointment or condescending approval of your moves towards isolation or integration. You're taught scantly at school that racism is about flashpoints, marches, riots, moments in history and figures in history, a boxed-off notion of race that includes Gandhi & MLK & Eichmann & Mandela that enables the ruling structure to safely kick race-hate into a touch-zone beyond itself, a problem for other countries, other times. What you learn fairly sharpish growing up coloured is that racism is a colder, more ever-present and steadily debilitating thing than that, a daily build-up, a constant sweeper of your legs and puller of the rug beneath yr identity, an endless, tiring, eternal part of your circumscribed mortal life. It happens so often you can't date it, or explain it any more than you can explain the air, the weather, the earth you're shoved down upon and that leaves its scars upon you. It fills the air, it can choke you, but of course, just like any other victim of a slow poisoning, you get used to it. You also learn to never talk about the way you feel, to keep things in, turn those experiences into an internal black wellspring that slowly seeps and hardens until it's an extra cancerous calcified layer of your skeleton, rattles and rubs inside your every move. In retrospect at least that early brush with racism was flagrant and outré and joyfully cruel and easy to respond to once I got my breath back – learned early that if you start getting wordy back, outfox those English (who seek to deny your Englishness) with your precocious command of their lingo, particularly the crueller swearier end of it, people tend to shut the fuck up, steer clear. That day, once the tears subsided, I realised that language has real power, committed myself to using it in my revenge. And to this day, the English language is the thing I love most about England, the thing I see as emblematic of what truly makes us great, our ability to absorb and take on influence from everyone we come into contact with.

As a strategy, pursuing Englishness to the point where I'm an extreme new form of Englander is something that eventually precipitates me becoming a critic, informs what criticism I offer.

My lifelong obsession with this country's history and people and language is not an attempt at bleaching myself with good citizenship, rather it becomes a search for an Englishness that's somehow more desirable, dignified and fair than the kind of Englishness I feel around me. At less distance from the horrors of empire pre-war English authors become a touchstone for me early on in my pre-teens, I find a rich seam of dissidence to England's nationalist mindset in literature, in books by Waugh and Orwell & Greene, deeper than I perceive anywhere else except the Specials who at the time boss my head, heart and Harrington. These authors mentor my precocious dissidence to the lie of Englishness the same way Burroughs, Genet & Crisp later oversee my lonely dissatisfaction with masculinity. Writers come to govern my life. By the time I'm a teenager and my Ernsford Grange memories are already fading I'm starting to realise that the hatred I got there was preferable in a way to the middle-class 'tolerance' I endure in the suburbs, that inclusion/exclusion so woolly and gaseous it's impossible to windmill against. UK racism I'm starting to discover, is less a tribal thing than it is an institutional thing, easy to spot in the skins and punks and the NF but more pervasive as a gentlemanly assumption of racial superiority that informs everyone from the kids who battered me in Ernsford Grange to the grown-ups who tell me I'm over-reacting the rest of my life.

In Ernsford also, all kinds of music is giving me worlds to hide amidst in my cubby-hole. Outside, I'm developing tricks of non-engagement, the right way to look at the ground whilst walking (to one side, not straight down), the right way to make that kind of walking tolerable (imagine you're being filmed) - I've always had cameras on me, either close up or hidden, there's one filming me right now, another bad old mental trick I pop into to take the pain from the situation a second. Outside, I've learned not to look people in the eye ever, even if you're talking to them, keep your gaze off to an angle so you can't read their revulsion in you, so they don't mistake eye-contact for an attempt to be liked or understood. Inside the house, inside myself, music is transforming me, pop, hip-hop, what happens after the charts, finger on condenser-mic pause button, whether it's Annie Nightingale or Peelie or the Velvets/Stones/T.Rex/Northern Soul my sister's friends are pinching from HMV & bringing home. And I'm starting to seek out Indian music on my own reconnaissance, seek out the Indian music that still thrills me, conjures worlds that to my parents are entirely familiar and part of their upbringing, worlds that to me are startlingly alien, that make me an alien by dint of being tied to them by birth, from birth. After you've been lashed by a racist 'incident', then slowly hipped to how that was only a flamboyant showcase of deeper, quieter, more unanswerable British assumptions, Indian music takes on a glow of resistance that even as an 8 year old you need and hold close. My sudden disappearance from the street, my retreat indoors is not a situation that makes me unhappy, not a grievance but a wedge between me and the world that I'm glad to cultivate and nurture. Precocious little fuck also lost now in classical music both western and eastern and, always always, my parents songs cos these are melodies and rhythms as blue and black as me, sounds I can't get anywhere else. 82 is the family's final move. The house I now live in. Hold it. What was that sound? That knocking? My friend? No. He, unlike the spirits that do walk these rooms, will give warning, will ring ahead. Ghosts, like love, only happen when you're not ready.

All houses are haunted, some by the living. In 2010 I walk the landing all summer, unable to write. Circumstances have landed me, lucky fucker & undeserving, back in the house I did all of my real proper growing up in, the house we moved to from Ernsford. It's the house I sluggabedded to school from, fags hid in a hole in a neighbour's fence, 2 B&H sucked down in the alleyway ensuring a wobbly-legged nicotine-numbed start to every day-of-learning. It's the house I started teaching myself in once it became clear that school weren't going to do that job properly for me. It's the house I fell back into after my first drink, first joint, first spell in the cells. It's the house that fronts the garden I fantasised in, cricket stump as AK-47, the world's leaders in helicopters hovering into the range & scope of my rotating-washing line gun turrets, the house that housed my dilettante armchair-revolutions and tripped-out epiphanies and gassed-up concussions. In that accelerated way that spoddy fucks, geeks & general malcontents do, I grew into the 150 year old man I am now in those teenage years, ready for death & other fictions and thinking I knew it all, promptly and on-schedule, by age 15, 1987, ready for Public Enemy and Throwing Muses and Young Gods and Melody Maker to propel me onwards. My school friends had girls and sports and games to play: my Saturdays and weekends were spent in libraries, accumulating sounds and words (Cov library & its lunatic 80s staff BIG SHOUT OUT), building my bedroom into a shrine to my immaculate impregnable taste. That bedroom is my kids bedroom now, that garden the one I find myself in throwing the same green-fingered shapes my dad did, shapes I never thought I'd fit.

After moving back in, a trip to the attic after enough weeks of plain walking-around-feeling-weird meant I rediscovered the EL3538, the tapes, the vinyl, the fiddly reels, and now I listen to this music in the same rooms I did 30 years ago and the air is thick with the past, spirits this and that side of death. Utterly unable to write. The other room, the front room, is where my dad would listen to music, pint of home-brew in hand, his own thoughts inaccessible to me, his emotional involvement clear whenever I strayed in'n'out of there. I sit in here, the back room, the room he was taken to die in so he could see the garden, the room I saw plenty of things I'd rather forget. Nigh on 30 years after I first heard it, and a good half-century-plus since these songs were composed and sung, I'm listening to a volume of

songs called *Marathi Chitrapaat Sangeet Volume 1*. Most of these
songs my dad had on various tapes patiently collated, after his
death committed to bin-liners in the loft. And whilst these songs
made my dad feel at home abroad in his new home in the 80s,
they simply made me, in 83 in this new house, feel strange, odd,
and aware that my own alienation from ALL cultures wasn't a
result of coincidence but down to it being encoded in my cells
helices. Melodies I couldn't explain, rhythms without time
conjured by the all-powerful multi-tracked voice above the
drone, one song in particular transfixing me then as it does now.
Another Hridaynath/Lata Mangeskar gem, another 1000 year old
libretto by the Saint Naneshwar who translated the Gita into
street-level Marathi from Sanskrit and that has the good sense to
know that God is a perfume, and his stink is everywhere. The
song's called *Avachita Parimalu* and is sung by Lata for the film
Amrutacha Ganu and featured heavily on the all-new cassette
tapes my dad would play whenever he had a chance, the old
reel-to-reel banished to the attic in 83, starting its 27 year wait to
be respooled and feel it's electrics hum into life again. Reels
creaking in the silence the Mangeshkars leave, it hinted to me,
before all the rest of what would be swimming through my 80s
managed to, that pop didn't have to be about verse-chorus-verse-
chorus and the last note didn't have to make you whole, or make
you smile. It taught me, on Lata's strange arcs of black-hearted
yearning, on the orchestra's disappearance into their own
shadows and echoes, that pop could just as easily be wonky as
symmetrical, could just as easily be hewn and moulded with an
almost Gaudi-like sense of nature and form, didn't have to add
up, could subtract down until it hit the negative realities of
dreams and death. It was, perhaps the first song I heard to
suggest that the synaesthesic hints & hits I'd got from music and
sound since the deaf-clinic, can actually be the intent of that
music, the ability to see a melody, see its limbs and their horrific
congress with the earth, see that spirit get up and crawl across

the room towards you. It chilled me as a child and does now in 2010. If you're watching it now on youtube, screens off if you can bear to be reminded of pure sound, and the pure visions that can come from it. Format matters see. I listen to these songs on vinyl and cassette but initially I heard them on quarter-inch reels my dad had bought over from Mumbai, recorded from his elder brothers' & friends' vinyl in India. The fag-packet-sized mic he used would occasionally be hooked up in Cov too and our voices recorded, now lost is a version of 'Where Have All The Flowers Gone', surreptitiously recorded by my dad and sung by me in the bath aged three. I'd spend hours with the Phillips machine, fascinatedly recording & playing back our voices, slowing myself down until I was as deep as my dad, speeding him up so I could imagine him as a child. That degenerated sound, the signal-loss from all that MOVING of this music from one format to another, is both an essential part of the immersion for me and also lacerbatingly reminiscent of those old days, even before the song starts, fondly remembered crackles and hiss, the sound of my dad moving the microphone towards the speakers back in his previous life, his previous home, his previous identity in our previous homeland. Putting a record on, playing a tape, are rituals, and the only one bar the sacred thread that two Bhramins as disparate yet close as me and my dad ended up sharing with any regularity. Some HMV Indian vinyl replaced Nipper the dog with a cobra (particularly on the classical/raga stuff that was an even bigger obsession for us than the film stuff), heavy shellac relics of the 'benefits' of empire, only accessible to that empire's subjects after the Raj retreated. If we've gone from objects that feel weightily full of sound to the dull convenient emptiness of data sprayed on discs or burned to hard-drives, then at least don't let your eye be distracted. Resist Stockhausen's correct insistence that 'the eyes dominate the ears in our time', try and give *Avachita Paramilu*'s ectoplastic reach some weight the only place you can any more, inside your head.

As, I think, with all music, you don't need to know what the lyrics mean. The reductive lie of word-exchange might blind you to your pre-lingual reaction which will be more accurate, honest, and open to an unpinned wonder. The weight of each concept is lost in such a process of retelling, the pure phonetics bereft of referent are clearer communication because they're something that anyone listening can understand and share – the words' antique import and meaning are unmoveable from the poet-saint tradition they emerge from without crumbling, or worse, being literally translated. Don't bother *reading* this most ancient mumbo-jumbo, but feel its force as sound, as invocation, as part of the song. Hinduism is the only faith on earth that should always come in inverted commas cos more than any other 'religion', Hinduism is about magic, is about the magic of rituals. That sacred-thread ceremony I shivered through in our living room, though mannered and tainted by inevitable Westernisation was still a real attempt to pass wisdom and knowledge on through the generations. At the temple on a Sunday every week, the music was dazzling, hypnotic, loud, communal – but the simplicity of the ceremonies at home always struck me deeper, the symbolic importance attached to rice, flowers, turmeric, flames and always the emphasis that the initiation had been passed on in one unbroken line for thousands of years. Whilst friends had confirmation gifts and christening cups and boy-scout badges, I had a thread of string, cheap as chips, beyond cost, fragile physically but unbreakable spiritually, something I was told that once received could never be renounced, was mine throughout life. No one could ever take it from me, I could never reject it, and that sacred-thread, long since lost as object but always alive in my memory, was always presented as perhaps the only permanent thing in an impermanent life. I'm discovering there might be more to my background than I'd been able to understand before, and more about god than simply the irrelevance of whether he exists or not. My dad's tapes and albums were the first songs that hinted to me that maybe sound was time-travel, that only music made time a dimension that could be stepped through, tapes that now suggest to me that maybe the future of music could be thousands of years old. In all Marathi songs, there was a linguistic umbilicus back to Sanskrit clearer than in Hindi or Urdu songs – Marathi as a language shares more ancient Sanskrit words and constructions than Hindi. This, in conjunction with Maharashtra's ancient singer-poet tradition, the fact our saints (Eknath, Gnaneshwar, Tukaram) communicated through poetry almost exclusively, and the strict rules of subject-matter and shape that govern Marathi song has always given golden-age (for me, 40s-60s) Marathi films a different intent and intrigue - for me entirely separate from Bollywood, entirely at odds with Bollywood's gleeful self-exploitation at home and abroad (entirely fittingly Marathi film is dwarfed by Bollywood now). Whether devotional or ritualistic (*Abhangs/Bhajans*), or romantic or plain randy (*Lavani*), ancient Marathi song's sense of purpose is clear, even if at our remove its exact place is enchantingly nebulous and nomadic. Bhajans are formless, improvised, based on scriptures or anecdotes from the lives of saints and focus in on an internal, personal journey to transcendental knowledge. *Abhangs* are less introspective, are meant to be sang by the community – the Marathi poet Tukaram specialised in them in the 17th Century as promo-tools for his Vakari movement, a religious revival that sought to put the emphasis back on a popular devotion to God rather than blind obedience to arcane ritual. The *Lavani* songs that also find a happy home in post-war Marathi film are a different kettle of juice altogether, and once I'd figured this out in the mid-80s it was like stumbling in on yr parents fucking.

"The main subject matter of the Lavani is the love between man and woman in various forms. Married wife's menstruation, sexual union between husband and Wife, their love, soldier's amorous

exploits, the wife's bidding farewell to the husband who is going to join the war, pangs of separation, adulterous love - the intensity of adulterous passion, childbirth: these are all the different themes of the Lavani. The Lavani poet out-steps the limits of social decency and control when it comes to the depiction of sexual passion."

K. Ayyappapanicker, Sahitya Akademi

Inevitable that when these ancient traditions, devotional and indecent, take themselves to the pictures in the 40s and 50s the results are pumped with independent pride, as well as touched with a new melodic. In comparison to the coy/whorish borrowed fantasy/chasteness of Bollywood, Marathi *'Shringarik Lavani'* (literally 'titillating songs') are genuinely erotic, useless to the repressed west, but entirely linked in with folk and classical-music traditions that are ancient, that link songs to times of the day and everyday activity, songs that understand how music must find a space in life to resonate, not pompously just boss reality into submission. No accident that in the new upwardly-mobile globalized Mumbai, Marathi songs, especially *Lavani*, aren't played much on the radio, spurned for their 'down market' feel. A fact exploited, as we'll see, by the scum in the Maharashtrian far-right as proof of a further erosion of Marathi (i.e. Hindu not Muslim) 'values'. *Lavani* songs bring the beats way more than Abhangs, that Dholki/Dholak thump that defies you not to dance – they're also harder to find in their raw state, before their motifs and modes got so comprehensively strip-mined by fledgling Marathi film. My dad had a few obscure 7"s and tapes of pure folk recordings of religious ceremonies that he'd play loud, extremely loud, first thing in the morning of a weekend, just massive massive beats covered in shouting. The *Lavani* use those beats & when you hear those beats, and when you hear the filth the women sing on top of it, s'impossible to resist - in comparison to the foreplay and teasing of current Bollywood pop, the nitty-gritty vulgarity of *Lavani* genuinely makes the earth move and the cheek blush. These aren't women singing and dancing with Western ideas of sexuality neutering it all, these are women singing and dancing in the heat of a pure passion, with the power and strength of a real lover in a real sexual moment, part animal, part out-of-body experience, part a body at it's zenith of pleasure and fusion with another. Too heavy for these times, too freely libidinous and informed by an ancient randiness for our modern days of fear and repression.

The use of old forms like *Lavani* & *Abhang* in Marathi film's fledgling days represents Maharashtrians pride in their past, a holding on to something old and local even as the medium used was a new exciting one that had a mass audience. It's also an act of desperation – as talkies emerged out of the Marathi silent era in the 30s it was to the travelling *Tamasha* shows (travelling plays & music thrown on in villages) & the more formalised tradition of *Sangeet Natikas* (operas & musicals) that cinema looked for inspiration to fill those soundtracks. The golden age of Marathi film extended from the 40s to the 60s, as a growing urban audience, the total lack of competition from television & the relative cheapness of a ticket meant it was the entertainment option of choice for an entire generation. As Bombay became Bollywood however, the shift in focus towards Hindi film (which could be marketed nationwide as opposed to just locally) meant that Marathi film became sidelined in the 70s & 80s, a marginalisation reflected in the slow quality-drop in Marathi film and Marathi song over that period. Always perennially boasting of its return, Marathi film is still a fairly insignificant part of the Indian film industry in 2011, pursued & hyped by politically-motivated Maharashtrians but failing to hold that central part in Marathi life it once did.

Odd thing for a critic to admit in these days where we're meant to be down with the kids (ignoring of course the fact that one of the joys of being a kid is being the most ferocious snob), but that precise dwindling in the source is undoubtedly part of

34

the elitist pull of this music. The withered petrifaction of contemporary Marathi song helps and focuses my blockheaded mind, particularly at a time when we're continually told how it's music criticism that is dead, over, not-needed, a time when every critic has to ask not only why the fuck they started but what in hell they're playing at carrying on. The disappearance of much Marathi song suits me perfectly. I'm glad the market's over. Gives me a static set of songs to renew on rather than an ocean of new songs to bemoan. If I'd had to keep up with Marathi song as well as Western pop I'd have been too exhausted in the late 80s cos that was the time my mind stopped smouldering and started burning for real. In 87 I'm walking through WHSmiths looking to kill another five minutes, a couple of bandit tokens in my pocket. I see a magazine called Melody Maker which has Public Enemy on the cover. I buy it and the rest of my life begins. Writers, popwriters, come to dominate my thoughts, map out my musical consciousness, give me a cannon and an anti-cannon to believe in & explore with clear, historically sure points of explosion and contraction. But always slightly resistant to that learning is this old music that even they don't write about, that I can only learn about when my dad or mum can be bothered to tell me what they're listening to. This music's reassuring yet revelatory place in my life always suggests to me that there's more to music than what the west has implanted in me and the further I've got into this music over the years the more I've realised that I have to shed what pop's taught me, I even have to shed what pop-writers have taught me, and start again with this music. That's why tonight the critic dies and my life starts again. This Marathi music is entirely resistant to the ideas of lineage and lists and order that pop criticism relies upon, the crit that maps my musical mind to a huge extent, but ends up in the stale dead ends I find myself in now. In the new millennium my default position is writers block, finding western music rotating around the same dead scraped-out ends, the criticism of it yawning forth reheated

35

fan-boy vomit and rag-mag smugness. Marathi music, with its roots so distant, its history so stalled and over and gone, is paradoxically way more intriguing and thought-provoking than pop's sham of forward-progress. Crucially, in its untranslatable mystery, it forces me to re-teach myself that music isn't simply 'all I care about', or 'my whole life maaan': listening, I remember that for whole chunks of the world music is as necessary every day as food, light, and shelter. Not just something you couldn't manage without, but something that makes you a human, makes you able to carry on being a human. Starts you from the dawn and gets you through.

What strikes me, rediscovering these songs in 2010 is how the entire Hindu 'faith' is a song passed on. We have no bible. No book. The Vedas, the Gita, the Upanishads – are barely texts to be analysed. Always a dead give-away to me that western attempts to understand Hinduism all attempt to codify it in texts with translations and commentaries and purports (usually the chance for the auslander evangelist or power-hungry mystic to dissipate mystery or ambiguity & crowbar in their own prescriptions and dogmas). Fatally misrepresenting Hinduism as a religion like all the rest, where books and the written word are finally the word of god. Hinduism makes no such claims for its works – it's all orally passed on poetry, turned into song to make it memorable to the illiterate. You don't have to believe in god. You just have to believe in the song. So what I oft-find in these soundtracks, soundtracks frequently from lost films I'll never get to see, is the exact opposite to a soundtrack. I hear not the backing to life or the recollection of image and celebrity that my parents enjoy, but life itself. My life. Everybody's life. Our separate lives. In the 80s, in the decade I spent between speakers and pages too indulged in time-wasting to have any room for God, the suggestion through pop songs in a foreign language that magic could be real, or that the dead could walk or that god wasn't a matter of reality but a matter of imagination was unsettling in a way the weirdest noise band could never be. Now, in 2010, it's unsettling to all my notions of who the fuck I am and what the fuck I'm playing at.

Criticism, its habits, can't help me with this stuff. In 2010 just as my trips to the attic are yielding this dusty plastic goldmine, I find myself genuinely facing the inability to write about *any* music any more. Paralysis, the way the great days we live in make you feel strapped down & force-fed to a gluttonous bloat. The texture of rotting celluloid captured on quarter-inch tape stuffed in suitcases & scrawled in indecipherable characters would easily be a fond retreat from the brashnesses of late-noughties pop – crucially beyond the pleasures of archaeology, 30 years later these songs all still sound like they're happening now, still speak for daydreams or a hope that's ageless and immortal. It couldn't have come at a worse/better time for me. In Spring 2010 I'm sent a Chess compilation of some of the greatest pop music ever made and can't say a word, and that coma of inarticulacy becomes an obsession in itself. For what possible response to 'Bo Diddley' can you have that would be better than listening to it? Go listen to those drums now. Comic voodoo heat untouched since and unencumbered by a coffin of pedals or any trick other than the unique joy of Bo himself. The more I hear the more I become convinced that the wrong people are making music in the West now, the wrong people getting those wrong people heard, more convinced that moments as head-shredding as Bo will never, could never, happen again so why bother listening to a form when it's mainly been so much pootling after the real fire has been laid down? How can you write about a culture when you're becoming convinced it has to roll itself back, learn the basics again – you're just an old fart continually bemoaning something you can't pin down beyond a loss of character in musicians, a loss of belief and ambition that you can't effectively critique cos it's all you feel about yourself. In such circumstances what becomes important aren't new sounds, but making the very act of making music in the first place a new thing, an effort disencumbered by the old leathered dreams of stardom and excess. The ongoing deadening the tinterweb has brought only makes those vintage souls all the more irreplaceably mysterious and untaintable by the spoddy manoeuvres of the pencil-pushing likes of me. You end up loathing that knowledge you can't shake – though I find myself fired up by the Marathi music I'm rediscovering how can I now write about the beats on *Airanichya Deva Tula* (another Lata-sung moment of bliss from the film *Sadhi Menasa*), or the weird sounds of *Om Namoji Adhya* (yet another Lata/Hridnyath ocean) without hearing Pram and Can and Moondog and a whole host of later discoveries hinted at? When it's nothing to do with them but the sounds of a bellows and an ironmonger, the unfolding and melodic problematisation of a drone until the drone disappears, less about avant-garde art or tin-pan-alley pop than it's about a village life and a spiritual self-immolation I never knew or can scarcely comprehend? There is, for me, at least some effort implied in my understanding of this music, whereas when I look at Western pop I can only feel my brain locking into the same old habits of categorisation, reference and curatorship. Looking at other writers' treatment of 'exotica' (i.e. anything from the 'commonwealth') for a route out I still read too many descriptions of oriental or African music practically gleeful in their realisation that 'Hey this sounds like [insert hip/laughable yet digestible western ref.point]'. In 2010, when the web seems to no longer be a launch pad into music, rather the ground we imprison it upon, it starts seeming more apposite to not only look deeper at the context and reasons behind eastern musics (at least to drag us away from the increasingly dwindling returns of the white/black conversation that is western pop) but also to, with some humility (foreign to most western perceptions) admit we can't just neuter this music with false lineages, by peripheralising it as an obscure point on maps we're over familiar with. We've got to stop seeing so much 'foreign' music as accidental simulacrum of the western forms we're familiar with but love it for the entirely alien things it can teach us, less a superficial re-cycling of its sounds than an internal absorbing of its structural oddity, the functions it serves in its native communities. We've got to rob our response of the easy options of amusement or our smug glow of geopolitical self-improvement and simply listen. We've got to see beyond the datedness & chuckle-icious cultural differences, contextualise our understanding/knowledge more but actually de-contextualise our listening, be more open to the music by being humble before it rather than arrogantly correcting it (or cheesily loving its incorrectness). In the face of something so instantaneously suggestive and wondrous as much of these tapes are, that's a difficult extra-effort, impossible of course given how we have so many years of western learning to overthrow and battle, but I'm totally bored with what's possible. In 2010 I crave our overthrow, our invasion, our surrender. I'm convinced we need to explore modes of listening rather than simply jazzing on the 'foreign-ness' of this other music. Because there's an infinity of it to explore and it's the only way out for us. Or for some of us, the only way back in.

This is what those tapes, pulled down from the attic, offer me the promise of: an ancient way to recast what it means to be a musician, and therefore what it means to write about music. When you think about Eastern concepts of music our current lazy-assed wankery in the west frequently gets exposed for the indulgent water-treading it is. The mathematical intervals of *Shruti*, India's tonal system, were worked out in prehistoric times and have an uncanny alignment with the frequencies & tones of Marathi film music. The seven-note *Swara*-scales always practised against a drone, each note linked not just to a part of the body but also to an animal sound the note is intended to mimic, can also be heard in fledgling Bollywood song . In classical music the ornamentation of those *Swara* notes is also formalised into the system of *Alankar*, the way a human voice (and by extension the instrumentation that came to mimic those voices in ancient Indian musical history) can slide between notes, fall like a monsoon rain and ascend like a spirit. The seasonal/temporal relativity of *Raga* (in Sanskrit, the word that means 'colour' or 'dye') is ancient , but as the major Indian music form & the template for composition & improvisation from which Indian classical music & film music springs it gives that music a discipline, a capability for experimentation within that discipline, unmatched by the West's more technologically-derived explorations. When my dad, belatedly started bringing back Tablas, sitars, harmoniums, dholkis, shehnais from his trips back home he also bought back books to learn from, books where the categories and confines of Indian music are explored in esoteric pages full of magic, science, and mystery. In comparison to the 'play from the heart' orthodoxy of the West, this was fearsome, foreboding shit for me to be finding out about music it was so easy to respond to. The production of rhythm or *Tali*, presented most explicitly that irreconcilable difference between theory and execution that's plagued my faltering understanding of Indian music ever since. *Taal* is a rhythmic cycle of beats with an ebb and flow of various types of intonations resounded on a percussive instrument – that much I understood but how could my Western-tutored pop mind cope with these weird beats, these patterns that only gained resolution after minutes of poly-rhythmic mathematical/magical exploration, rhythms with their own verbal notation system taught on to musicians through phonetic mantras. This was, and is, mind-boggling stuff, suggestive not just of the inherent complexity of Indian folk-music, but also the wider oddity of being a musician in India. This isn't something you do because you want to be a star. This isn't a life you commit to for the trappings. This is never merely a hobby. This is an ancient discipline that requires years, decades, of steady & relentless mental & spiritual commitment. Western pop says anyone can make it, relies upon the myth of the meteoric overnight rise from local talent to global superstar. Indian pop says the same can happen, but demands more than simply hard-work, the ability to publicise yourself – it requires the ability to time-travel, to surrender to a system in order to find your artistic and personal liberation. This closed book of intrigue and science was usable by a money-making young Bollywood, but the motives of the composers and singers behind that young Bollywood were clearly more complex than fame, motives and impulses millennia older than even the empires and confederacies that the new independent India emerged from. Reading about such time travel, listening to the products that had been made from it gave me that arm across the window again and again in the 80s, that sense of an ancient security that still holds me, still stops the ring of steel from belching forth fire across my temple. And if the western music that once fired me is starting to sound like a ghostly emanation from a past of wholeness my broken self can never recreate, this Indian music, based on entirely different ideas of wholeness offers a chance to rebuild the horrified, looking-back, trapped person I am now. Like I said, a matter of survival, then as now. When I first moved to this house I quickly came the realisation that my soon-come teenage years were not gonna be about fighting for the right to party, but fighting for the right to not party and to bleeding well concentrate. Happy chappy. Miserable bastard. Serious times the 80s, and that's often forgot. No-one but ourselves to look to. Realising that, like our parents, we are also, whether we want to be or not, pioneers.

Chapter 3

The A-Z Of Fear

"I never heard anyone say, when I grow up, I want to be a critic"

Well, even Richard Pryor can be wrong. The aggravation that had been building since a young age, combined with an intense shyness, and an equally intense sense of language as performance & defence meant I had to be a some kind of scribe, hell, it's what my name means. As I was to discover late on in the 80s writers, the best writers, didn't just tell you what you could be listening to, they came to occupy a deeply intimate place in your life. To the point where you felt them overseeing your choices, to the point where they open the world up to you. See, you can be eight and sobbing down by the VG supermarket after an unkind word and a smack in the face from a passing peer and realise that England is a bitch. It takes you a little longer to realise how that bitch can fuck you over, problematize you forever. White skin so pure. Black skin so pure. You? Denied cool. Always the wannabe. The way Indians get portrayed by the English in my still-unfolding formative years is always somehow needy, wanting in, fatally and laughably unable to be cool. Basic point about 70s & 80s Britain – if you were part of an ethnic minority your life wasn't just unrepresented anywhere else, it was a life almost led in subterfuge to the mainstream, a mystery to school friends, street-friends, teachers, everyone bar you and your fam. Its mundaneity wouldn't surprise anyone, but if you were Asian it felt like black *and* white hated you, and when you're not surrounded by Asians who hate back with any kind of intelligence you're left feeling kinda soft, unarmed. That 'Mind Your Language' quiet acquiescence in our own ridicule was all we saw of ourselves in British culture and even those scant glimpses of shame were only when we weren't simply invisible, out of the press (apart from the usual 'issues'/'problems'), off the telly, never ever on the radio. It's taken fucking ages for that to change, for Asians to present anything other than a wheedling subservience to a white culture they want in on. I'd say that only in the past 5 or 6 years have Asians genuinely become another part of the furniture on TV, have been able to simply *be* without being attached to some exotica or issue (arranged marriage/cruel marriage/violent-marriage, still to this day Asian culture has a handy displacement function for a white culture that needs it's 'subtler' misogyny diffused – 'Asian Paedophilia Gangs' are the latest deodorant of choice I believe). Even now, it's rare for an Asian to be represented without the comforting attachments of food and Bollywood to swiftly attach themselves – in the entire sub-genre of Anglo-Asian reminiscence I still find far too much self-deprecation, too much jollity in juxtaposition, far too little anger. Asian anger and refusal of Britain's head-patting condescension, as I found later, has a history that stretches back to the 30s in the UK. A history that wends close to my home too – one of the first Indian Workers Associations to be created in Britain was created in Coventry in 1938, Coventry the ever politically-agitated city that gave birth to 19th & 20th century political figures as diverse as Mo Mowlam, Tomas Mann & leading neo-Nazi Colin Jordan. More concerned with worldwide socialist revolution and Indian Independence than the trade-unions that barred Asian membership, the fledgling Coventry IWA meetings were attended by Udham Singh, a member and frequent speaker, a firebrand who went back to India to complete the successful assassination of General Dwyer in 1940, revenge for the Jallianwala Bagh massacre. To this day in Cov, the kabbadi tournament that takes over the rugby-ground every year is named the Udham Singh tournament, in honour of this Marxist-Leninist agitator who called Cov a home and would end his days in Brixton & Pentonville nicks, hanged under the name Ram Mohammad Singh Azad (a taken name he adopted to demonstrate his transcendence of race, caste, creed, and religion). Nehru said Singh had 'kissed the noose so that we [the Indian people] could be free', Gandhi refused to honour him– what was bizarre to me was that this was a guy who lived and worked & rabble-roused in the same areas I grew up in, down the road from the Courtaulds factory my dad worked in. As a teenager craving this knowledge, I had to dig deep for it in the footnotes and forgotten byways of books no-one reads any more, it was a history of Asian resistance to discrimination that was revelatory and inspirational to me, accompanied with the angry realisation that I'd had to find out about it for myself, that no-one was teaching me or telling me this stuff. I can't stress how formative that lack of presence in the culture was, how what I was learning was clashing so much with our cultural representation, how much it meant for black and brown in the UK when you heard LKJ or the Specials or Lenny Henry on the telly or radio, those rare special moments where the whitewash lifted. The whitewash hip-hop was to truly and finally lift from my vision.

Starved of a culture I could truly call my own but at least dimly aware of a history I wasn't being taught, by the time I turned 11 I was primed for hip-hop to come stomping into my life and offer revelation and revolution. It did, via 'The Message' played on Mercia Sound's morning show as I sat in the back of a blue Hillman Imp (next to the engine). I remember it as the moment my teenage years started, ordering my mum to turn the radio up at the top of a snowy Gulson Road, waiting for the lights to change and hoping the handbrake held. Every moment since leads back to it. Rap was never purely the vicarious thrill as writ about in the music press to this day, hip-hop was a bolt from the blue that seemed to me, still does, to be the only music to accurately map something approaching my consciousness, splattered and splayed by a dizzying array of sources, leaving me

44

seething with questions as to how that revolutionary everything-is-usable mindset could help me. Even with rap though, it was still engagement with a culture you never saw on the screen, only heard sporadically. Prince was more visible and he became my next obsession. Asians could imagine looking like him. But actual real Asian folks you never saw ANYWHERE *except* where the piss was being taken. The stereotypes that 70s/80s telly threw out about Asians were living lessons that if you're told to be a good sport it tends to be for your humiliation, if you're told it's 'harmless fun' it's guaranteed to touch-down at playground-level with no fun, and plenty of harm. It introduced you to the twin concept that not only can they take the piss out of you as much as they want, if you dare to raise a single voice against it, you'll be lambasted for over-reacting, spoiling the fun, 'thinking' about it all too much.

As for pop, bar Freddie Mercury, who as with so much, never *exposed* himself, we were nowhere, absolutely nowhere. How could we be? Black musicians, though frequently marginalised, were at least part of English pop culture, increasingly were taking that step from peripheral figures to front men and women. Asian musicians were seemingly nowhere to be seen. According to pop, no matter what our moves in real life, we were still to be drawn into the first faltering steps of 'integration', that dance with the other wherein the other gets rendered palatable. And this lingered long after black musicians could feel confident as figureheads – deep into the 80s Asians were still persona non-grata in Western pop. Bereft of anyone from my background answering my turmoil, hip-hop like Public Enemy & Ice Cube & Ice T from the States, and Gunshot, and Ruthless Rap Assassins & Black Radical Mk II from the UK filled in the gaps in my knowledge, pointed me towards a wealth of reading and listening that finally started answering some of the questions I was having about racism, the white power structure, the history of hate that I felt we were still always living through, even as mainstream culture was pretending those wars were over. It was still however, mainly black culture, whether reggae, dancehall, dub or hip-hop, that seemed to at least be addressing this. The Asian pop music I got to hear that wasn't decades old, looked & sounded identical to the West's 80s aspirational models, seemed to have no impetus bar a desperation to sit alongside western pop. The first time I saw myself or my kind of radginess repli-cated anywhere was in 94 when Fun-Da-Mental happened, even later in the 90s when Cov-born Punjabi MC bought bhangra to the charts it had that feel of novelty-single, like Whitetown, like a brief foray into the mainstream before the usual retreat back to our own undergrounds (and so it proved). The fact that Asian music is now reduced down to catch-all titles like 'desi' and predominantly ignored by the pop mainstream bar the odd stolen loop/vocal re-emphasises just how little Asians are repre-sented in pop, just how 'foreign' this music still is. The abiding assumption being that we're timid, would rather stick to our own – only in UK hip-hop, a music massively marginalised, do I see equal participation of Asians – really reflective of how the Bollywood pop that is many Asians primary pop experience doesn't NEED mainstream acceptance in the UK to survive, it has a population of a billion in India to cater to. That ability for many Asians to now feel confident enough to simply pursue their native tastes in the land they've migrated to means that Asian culture is to a large extent still invisible in the UK, keeps itself to itself. But that comfort & ease in inconspicuousness was not the way my parents raised me, and not a tactic that was possible for me growing up: that retreat into a 'native' narrative was impos-sible when Marathi song was itself on the retreat in the Indian 70s (bulldozed out of Bollywood in favour of Hindi films that could appeal to the whole nation), when I was being so gleefully saturated in a Western culture I saw no reason I shouldn't belong to, a culture that in pockets and peripheries of the past and present ,offered me the rebel strain and political bite I found so lacking in mainstream pop whether white *or* Asian. My parents, and my sister were crucial: they were cool, they stepped off, let me read, pushed Sivanandan and Ellison and Malcolm X and Marx my way, let me a little loose from the strict career-minded strictures that made so many of the other Asian kids me and my sister met seem so weirdly part of some pre-program, armed with futures that simply didn't interest us. For me and my sister, an older Western culture of art and rebellion spoke more clearly to our dreams than present-day Asian culture's emphasis on (teenage snort of derision) 'entertainment' and conformity. We turned to our own kind and they were from a different planet. They were eager to please.

All our teenage lives we were introduced to kids who ostensibly should've been like us. Like them, we'd grown up with Marathi parents, like them, those Marathi parents tried to keep their roots intact. Unlike us however, their parents seemed concerned only with one kind of fitting in – the ability to reach a point where you could make money, become a 'professional', economically earn your place. In order to maximise their kids 'competitiveness' their parents controlled pretty much every facet of these kids lives, from the books they read to the telly they watched to the music they listened to. Their parents were always worried about their kids growing up 'too English', kept their offspring's cultural inputs as withered and limited as their own, set their parenting ambition as churning out clones of themselves, kids who'd end up as nervously ambitious and greedy (and usually deeply and offensively Hindu-nationalist in their politics) as them. My parents watched as me and my sister became gobby little lefty freaks and pretty much gave up on any notions of us fitting in by the time we were in our teens. From then, we were free. They allowed me the breathing space to learn that you can either get angry and sad, or angry and proud, and you'll often get both, allowed me the dawning discovery that that crinkle-cut chip on my shoulder and this pain in my heart are touchstone, launch pad and cul de sac inescapable. In startling contrast, the kids we were introduced to were sensible, never gave their dimwit parents the credit of being able to cope with disobedience, barely listened to Western pop, slavishly stuck to the Marathi music that was all the music their parents supplied, if they supplied music at all. Art was not a lucrative enough aspect of life to waste time on when there were qualifications to earn, studies to commit to, doctors and lawyers and businesspeople to become. Painfully straight-laced people I felt even less solidarity with than most of the white folk I knew.

But then, I'm getting angrier as the 80s roll on. I almost entirely blame my school. I'm put in a grammar school as a toddler then asked later if I want to continue to another fee-paying grammar. Scared of anything new, I forego the opportunity to drop out and swim with the kids I know down the street & continue to be privately educated at monetary cost to my parents, and lasting social cost to myself. A fatal, yet apolitical, misjudgement on my part and perhaps my parents also, that only really starts biting when I realise that the 'tolerance' of the middle-classes is the worse possible nurturing ground for anything other than a constant debilitating hatred of whitey I'm yet to fully shake. I develop this hatred because I went to King Henry VIII school in Coventry for 11 years of my life. Take a stroll up Warwick Road from the Station and you'll see it. Fucking ridiculous building with a facia that looks like a medieval castle, augmented with modernist blocks, reflecting its old-boys-network pretensions and it's nasty streak of Thatcherite drive. Rich kids & posh kids & just about making-it kids went here, parents suckered by its pretence at being a public-school in the Rugby mould, kids dazed at the Victorian parochialism that went on behind that façade. Jerry Dammers and Philip Larkin were the only alumni I ever cared about. We had houses, house-ties, delusions of jolly-hockey-sticks grandeur, a teaching staff composed nearly-entirely of paedophiles, child-beaters, fundamentalist Christians, classical scholars and right-wingers. My sister, 3 years older than me, was part of only the 2nd female intake. By the time I was in & already developing the scruffiness, terror-of-PE & avoidance of work that would blight my school-life forever we were 2 of about 4 Asian kids in a junior school of about 400. When we passed the 11 plus and made it into the senior school we were 2 of about a dozen Asian kids in a school of nigh-on 800. Racism was, as with most schools at the time and to this day, a daily occurrence, something you went home and cried about until those tears could harden into a response. My response was always verbal, never thrown a punch in my life, and (enough times to not get down about it) it was a response *better* than theirs & *faster.* Be nastier back. On my first day in the junior school aged 6 I called another kid a 'fucking bastard' and was dragged in front of my one-armed Jewish-homosexual head teacher (there were nice guys there in amidst the Nazis, like I say, a strangely populated place), bollocked, and told to write a 2 page essay on the word 'bastard', it's meanings, it's uses, and why I shouldn't have said it. I plagiarised it from an obscure safely irretrievable source (ahhh Readers Digest Books, how much I owe you), a trick I've used ever since. Through those 11 years at that institution I was lazy, but finding ways to survive. The bored & bullied becomes the bully, lashes downwards & draws tears from those who won't fight back. Steady consistent theft and defacement at the library, on report and in detention elsewhere, never a prefect, mainly dossing around, later on drinking in lunch-hour, I got through. I recall sitting on my last day there dreaming the whole panorama of gym and playing fields and chemistry lab aflame, teachers corpses riddling the walkways, fellow students running screaming, a revenge too good not to keep in the imagination. Violent thoughts, never actual violence cos I'm too much of a coward and too smart to want a beating.Two of my teachers ended up with their paedophilia outed, one committed suicide, one wrote Christian tracts about how the bible insists that children "must be sexualised" and taught my sister that "the IQ of black Americans was lower than that of black Africans because they were the stupid ones who had got caught for the slave trade". Another teacher forbade any involvement in relief for Africa because Ethiopia was a 'communist country'. Another threw objects at you, sent you to first-aid if he drew blood. Another smacked you in the face, another took secret photos in the showers, another popped pills, another sexually-initiated male & female pupils he took a fancy to - you learned these eccentricities, mind boggling at the auld-England that created them, the 'best days of your life' (don't worry kids, they ain't) a fucking nuts cartoon populated by ancients of the ancient schools, incidents of cruelty and stupidity & vindictiveness too numerous to mention, far too many teachers hankering for the brutal days of yore, the teaching that had battered them into the weird shapes they were in. You got through despite it, and the English teachers were alright, mainly hippies (the women) and old queens (the men). Started to discover in English, that I wasn't bad at writing, could occasionally be moved enough, (like my Uncle Abba especially blown away by Shakespeare) to come up with unique responses. Music teaching, with the advent of GCSEs is moving from the historical (which I excelled at with my at-home/library spod-u-like development of knowledge about classical music) to the practical (which I'm shit at) but music, by 85, is becoming the only thing alongside literature that I care about. I hit the Marathi stuff hard in the mid-80s partly because of the sheer grain of it – it's scratchy and atmospheric in an era in which I find it hard to like the sounds bands are making. In the Live Aid years (which is a sound doubtless being rehabilitated as I speak, some earnest defender of big 'orrible echoey drums and a whole mess of fretless fuckwittery tweeting 'It Bites' videos long into the night) I go backwards in all music. Un-hiply, I listen to nigh-on purely 60s and 70s music for two years instead of Nik Kershaw & Climie

Fisher (sozboz), and what current Indian pop I hear in the 80s is just as shite as the western pop it's ripping from. I'm engaging in nostalgia for an India that perhaps never existed, the scratching search for roots when your DNA is forged 5000 miles away from your birthplace – crucially I'm in free-fall at the realisation that, hold on, I ain't gonna fit in ANYWHERE.

A growing realisation that I don't even feel at home being an Asian, because Asians I know beyond my own family have a sense of community, meet up, large groups, places and spaces and surety. In contrast, we're seemingly a community of four, eight at a stretch if you include blood-tied folk from London. The language my parents speak, Marathi, is spoken between them and them only. When we go to Foleshill, Cov's main Asian area, hearing my mum twist her mouth into the consonants of Hindi and Urdu even I, remorselessly and lazily uni-lingual, can tell the difference. In India I'd be living in a state of 100 million people, the second most populous in the country. In England, Maharashtrians number nearly-none in the 70s and 80s. We weren't part of that wider influx of Gujaratis from Uganda that had Enoch frothing at the gob, although the hatred he touched on has shadowed me always, and always will. At school, I'm realising that the middle-classes have just as venal hatreds in their hearts, but have the power to construct glass ceilings of sociability underneath them, out of them, closed circles you look foolish even trying to enter – I hid away, with a couple of close friends who ended up leaving me. By the 6th form I was on my tod, and folk steered clear, and that was fine by me.

That sense of being an alien, that self-aggrandizement inevitable to the slightly pompous teen, was exaggerated for me everywhere I went, even if I sought a community to belong to. In the 80s I don't walk down the streets of ghettos like Hillfields or Foleshill or Longford feeling at home. Sure I feel safer, I feel like I can disappear/show myself easier, I don't feel folk crossing the road to avoid me like I do everywhere else, but I know I don't belong there either, know I don't see my family's curious features mirrored anywhere. The A to Z of fear that is created deep inside your brain if you're black or brown is getting fully mapped out for me, the streets you can't go down, the places you can't walk in, the unofficial lines of segregated geography that are laid down young and stay forever. Sure, maybe paranoia but racial paranoia is at least, safety. I can walk into the Standard Music Centre, the Asian-record shop down Foleshill road and feel as alienated as I do in HMV or Our Price but I can feel unnoticed, I can sit in the barbers getting my chrome dome shaved drinking heavy sweet cardamom tea and listen to the conversation and not understand a single word but for once not feel under observation. Race, when you're one of only about five Asian kids in your entire school, is important, creates and moulds your consciousness and the cut of your jib in a vintage disappearing way. Gives you a conflicted sense of wanting to vanish and wanting to make as big a noise as possible, hide out and try and figure out who the fuck you are but also stamp your greenhorn incongruity on the cosmos. There's a small rack of Ustad Bismillah Kahn & other raga maestros in the music shop. That's where I go. The medallion-man clichés of the Bollywood sound-tracks that cover the walls leave me absolutely cold, as they still do, because that shit could be from anywhere, made by anyone, piped into any shop in any city on earth. Even by the midst of the 80s I can hear that its aspirations are becoming almost entirely westernised, entirely globalized to the point where the specific and local is subsumed in the welter of Western expectation, I can hear it losing the universality and strangeness of old Marathi cinema-song, losing its unique prehistoric suggestions and unmediated wonder. So just as I'd rather listen to the Velvets and the Stones and Motown comps while the 80s rolls its Burtons sleeves up and back-combs itself into grisly big shapes, by 1985/86, in contrast to the clear commercial space that Bollywood pop is ravenous for, I opt to lose myself in those old tapes, that

52

old classical vinyl that even then is becoming a relic of an India gone. Snobbishly distasteful of the new Indian pop, this old stuff keeps yielding a sub-cellular glow I can't explain which you could call 'belonging', a racial memory that cuts beyond language. Something to do with the beats, with the fact that Marathi movies of the golden age so often fantasised a rural Maharashtrian idyll that my parents, like so many of their gener-ation, had abandoned for a city life in Mumbai or even further afield. Songs that make you wonder about what could've been, what you'd be if your folks had stayed in the village, how out-of-synch you are with your destiny as is anyone who escapes the world they were born to, to step and stumble out into another. Out of synch as is anyone who's walked on those black beaches barefoot and finds themselves grown up and trudging through a substance called snow that they'd only read about before. In such a torment of shattered identity, Amitabh Bachan breakdancing wasn't gonna cut it as glue to repair me, as anything I could get behind or get together with. Hip-hop stepped in and gave me a way my broken-ness couldn't just be lived with, but lived FROM, could become the ground I could grow up above. I can trace an awful lot back to 'Yo Bum Rush The Show' and Public Enemy because they introduced me to thinking about race without fear, to realising that a head seething with questions doesn't have to find answers or hide out and pretend it's OK. By the time, through PE, I'd got into the music press and a whole lot of other stuff through that conduit; I've been bent out of shape severely. Got put forward for Oxford & Cambridge. Fucked up the exam cos people like Chris Roberts & Simon Reynolds & David Stubbs & The Stud Brothers have brilliantly fucked up my life as later Simon Price & Taylor Parkes would, end up ranting about situa-tionism in response to a rather anodyne question about the Duchess Of Malfi, unrepentant when my appalled English teachers lambast me for my foolishness.

Learning by now, is something I take from everywhere except

school, something I do everywhere except the classroom. I cannot emphasise enough just how much the magazine Melody Maker meant, and still means to me. Every Wednesday morning, it was my education, my inspiration, my launch pad into the world. It seems strange now, the idea that something as transitory & supposedly ephemeral as a magazine could exert such a collosal hold over someone, no matter how ripe for takeover I was back then. But even though the paper it was printed on could've wrapped up yesterday's chips, the words and images that were printed were titanic, huge, and life-changing, as etched in my memory now as they ever were. It wasn't something you could say about all music magazines, only the Maker. It was special, a unique collection of individuals working at peak power. Not only was the music that the Maker introduced me to a revelation, it also picked out the sources I should be studying, the films and books that surrounded the culture, the writers and theorists I had to follow, every piece threw down hints to a thousand other things you could explore. In contrast to today's endless music-crit efforts to be down with the kids, the Melody Maker never ever felt like it was talking down to you, only across, only with both the humility and conviction strong enough to allow you as a reader to catch up, to try and understand, pursue your own avenues. The people who wrote for the mag, and the photographers who snapped for it became obsessions for me as deep as the music they sent me towards and shot: Simon Reynolds' mindblowing conflation of modern theory and noise, David Stubbs' scabrous humour and deep intuitive use of the English language's vulgarian power, Chris Roberts' enormously stylish mix of poetry, suggestion and romance – these people, and many others, ended up, even though they seemed to be living enviably connected lives in the big smoke, massive shadowy presences in the life of this little fuck-up from Cov, overseeing my life and it's choices, yaying or naying every decision whether sartorial or aesthetic, popping off a myriad directions your head could be splattered to. Your heart would rush of a Wednesday, knowing that at some point you'd be picking up the newest copy, my room was a place where the photos of Tommy Sheehan, Steve Gullick and Joe Dilworth would end up on my wall, the writings of the Stud Bros and Carol Clerk and Paul Oldfield and Jonh Wilde & Paul Mathur & Jon Selzer & Simon Price scoured, re-read, re-absorbed. These were writers who seemed to know everything about music, but crucially they were writers who clashed, disagreed, and had something to say about how pop should and could be, and that opened up a vital space whereby you could start thinking for yourself. They were cool, often cooler than the musicians they wrote about. In stark contrast to the needy, party-crashing tactics of today's press, these were writers stylistically bold enough to exist in their own space and drop their own atmospheres onto you & into your life whenever you started reading them. After a while you could spot them a line in, their voice, their hold on your heart and head. Even when I leave school (and after a summer in which my mum burns all my old copies saying they're a 'fire-risk' – still not forgiven her) and end up studying at York Uni their weekly transmissions transfix me, new people like David Bennun, Cathi Unsworth, Andrew Mueller, and particularly two writers I'd come to call friends, Simon Price & Taylor Parkes, providing me with a weekly dose of rocket-fuel to the skull, always funnier and faster and sharper and more generously honest to their own dreams and delusions than any other kind of writing I'd ever read. Writers, you felt, who had read, who had also been separated a little from their peers thanks to the big over-heated brains they were lugging around their whole life, the mad amount of listening and learning they'd, like you, wasted their adolescence with. I owe that paper & the saints and angels and devils who wrote for it, everything. Finally free at uni from the middle-classes and able to reconnect with the white working class my schooling separated me from, the white working class who've rightfully taken the piss out of my poshness ever since, I find in English lessons that I'm surrounded by stuck-up wankers, realise I ain't gonna get a fucking job out of this. Decide seminars and lectures with these twats are less important than the pub. Also getting into a frenzy about music and writing, waste my words in love letters, waste my mind with 9-bars and shabby slaggishness, only able to listen to Indian music back at home in Cov when trainfare can be scraped up.

Videos now make it possible for me to watch the films these songs come from but I end up watching with my eyes shut. When I hear the stunning *Akheracha Ha Tula Dandavat* (sung for the film *Maratha Tituka Melvava* in 64 by Lata with her sister Usha providing 'echo') I'm amazed to discover that Lata also composed the music under the male pseudonym Anand Ghan, but when I look at the screen, all is out-of-synch, mouths open to silence, shut to be given voice. Eventually that starts suiting me fine too cos I feel out of synch, I feel there's a mismatch between the simple stories & bucolic idealism of the films and the suggestive wonder of the music and sounds. Hearing the wonderful song *Jithe Sagara Dharnimilte* sung by the exquisite Suman Kalyanpur (a Bengali singer relocated to Mumbai) the out-of-synchness reverberates even stronger, I realise that both Suman & me are born out-of-synch with our place, displaced to somewhere we will always be a visitation in. The composers, as revealed on the credits, start to become an obsession, because unlike my parents, I don't associate these songs with the experience of watching movies, I associate these songs with closing my eyes and letting the pictures come unbidden. Names like Sudhir Phadke, a great classical & playback singer in his own right and composer of some of my favourite Marathi songs, Shrinivas Kale who's hits have been part of Marathi film for 60 years now, the genius Hridaynath Mangeshkar who's *Koli Geets* (fisherman's songs) redolent of the Konkan roots of my mum – these were people who's individual styles were unmistakeable once you knew which songs they'd wrote, but who were almost vanished in terms of their persona and presence unless you lived in India, unless you scoured the sleeve notes of what vinyl you had and hassled your parents for instant translations. People I wanted to find out about but whose lives were shrouded in obscurity and modesty – as a vintage pop fan and a fan of vintage Marathi song there was a powerful mismatch between those western artists who pushed their egos right at you, and these quiet genii who almost seemed to want to disappear, letting other singers and actors take the spotlight armed with their songs. Partly you put it down to that meekness you so wanted to destroy in yourself, later you realised it was more laced in with the entirely different notions of what it was to *be* a musician that prevailed in the East.

I'm aware in the 80s, that the move I'm making on Indian music is as squalid & fearful & reactionary as that of a rare-groove fan on black music, or a classical-music fan who refuses to listen to anything later than Brahms. I was listening to exclusively 'old' Indian music, to the denigration of what was actually contemporary Indian pop in the 80s, a retro-fixated snobbery that mirrored my distaste for contemporary western pop. Partly it's pre-emptory resistance to a perceived patronisation -'Indian' pop as perceived by the English as I grow up is nigh-on entirely those pale imitations and painful malapropisms of contemporary western pop that reassures and ratifies a white industry's control of what we hear, their artistic 'right' to that control. The camp failure, the Bengalis-in-platform stereotypes: the ephemeralisation that always accompanies the designation 'exotic' means half the planet's music, of which India is a substantial part, has always only been afforded the hipster dabbling that characterises most people's 'foreign' listening. That mistreatment of non-white music by the white-dominated music industry, that I see in the misrendering of hip-hop in the mainstream media as well as the complete ignorance of Eastern musics across the entire media, has started to really get stuck in my craw by the late 80s. The germs of realising that maybe, at the Maker, in my daydreams, there'd be a place for me and my problems. For me, as primarily a hip-hop fan, the way hip-hop was written about often seemed guided by the same mistaken sense of the music only gaining respect when it told you what you already knew, reified the same old Stagerlee/insurrectionist stereotypes (i.e. had encoded within it the reassuring narrative of black FAILURE). The revolutionary possibilities of hip-hop not just as music or message but as way of thinking about the world seemed to be entirely ignored. By the time Uni coughs me out in 93, I'm fucking seething. Six months in to a dole-life I have no desire to ruin with work I write a letter and another stage starts. The letter that got me in at Melody Maker was about precisely the frustration I felt at white treatment of black music, and after hired I've banged on about little else since, because still deep into the new millennium black music simply doesn't get the same treatment as white, still is hidebound by clichés of instinct that refute intellect. At *Melody Maker* I was allowed, finally, to vent, and encouraged by fellow writers (particularly my reviews editor Simon Price and the guy who initially spotted my letter, Taylor Parkes) to follow and feel fearless in that line of attack. I can't imagine any print editor right now being like that – monomanias, obsessions, ideas of how pop SHOULD be rather than simply reporting on what pop was, were actively encouraged at the Maker, visions competitively perfected, your journey through pop and yourself not only allowed but *respected*, a uniquely joyous place to work whose sacrifice & destruction by cruel commerce and evil-plans enacted by utter utter cunts would be one of the most traumatic episodes of my life. Ahem, don't get me started – at least *at the start* my intent as a critic was always to dis-avail people of the timidity and temerity they had for black music, this idea always that in liking black music you either wanted to *be* black or are taking a cheap holiday in other people's misery. For me, in the early 90s, that misery required no holiday-ticket to visit, stepping out my front door or staying in and watching telly you could see that racism was as alive and well on the streets of the UK as it was anywhere else. Hip-hop was the only music coming from a minority or immigrant perspective, the only music suggesting a cannon beyond the usual rock names, and the only music saying anything politically. Its treatment as a fad, hype, or technique rather than art form seemed to me utterly incommensurate with the lessons you could learn from it lyrically, the places cosmic and street-level that it could propel you to in the space of a syllable or a loop. It was musical armour, a new shape to throw back at the cosmos. Any person in a minority looking for music that mirrored their own chaos was listening to rap music in the late 80s & early 90s. For all its avowed aggression & stridency, it was actually the confusion of it, the power it gained from the piling up of that confusion in sound & word, that made it such an essential soundtrack to the blistering tension and rage of being who you were.

As part of a minority you've always got too much on, frequently too much on your mind, an extra level of negotiation with yourself and others that simmers and seethes along with everything you do. It's exhausting, when a minority within a minority doubly so, when a minority within the minority of a minority well . . . you can imagine – the pride my auntie thought my mum should have in her racial-rarity found it's inverse in the anger I felt stranded out in Cov a might-as-well-be million miles away from anything I could call my roots. My response as the 80s ended & the 90s began, inspired by the writers who every Wednesday for 75p were blowing my mind, was to examine how things seemed through my prism, make sure I was able to express myself through voracious reading and shameless plagiarism, developed the trick of saying things other people wish they had said. Were I an arrogant cock, which I am, I'd admit that that's a trick handy for being a critic; it's also a trick that in the wrong bored juvenile & cowardly hands can turn you into a nasty cunt at times, a verbal bully. Angry little bastard, using Western pop as taught me by *Melody Maker* & others to assuage or amp that anger, aware that much of my life would be spent as some kind of irritant, yet more unsure of exactly how that inner-volcano could be safely unleashed. University was even more loneliness and aggravation and the beginning of drink and drugs as lasting solution but for real calm, back in Cov, for a sight of another way that nothing else offered, I tried sometimes to imagine how my parents listened to these songs the first time as the old TDK reels rotated again. In the village, surrounded by jungle (ironically when I listen to Ustad Allah Rakha Kahn or V.S Jog in 92/93 I hear jungle-d'n'b prefigured polyrhythmically), travelling cinema set up amidst the trees and snakes and monkeys and these astonishing songs coming singing through the thick forest air. I've only been to India twice. Once when I was a month old, of which I recall nothing. Then once again in 1982. I hoped to afford to go again but never did – but as I face-down adulthood at the end of the 80s I could at least say I've been to that jungle, seen what I dreamt, heard and felt the hum and energy, been part of an ancient routine, dodged army ants and snakes and lizards in my mum's village and my dad's village, noticed I am never stared at yet feel terrified in the roaring Mumbai streets that became both their homes, came home to Cov, my home, shaken and shocked at my own precarious identity. Able to realise that perhaps I should never ever talk race with the white folk, they simply will never ever get it, and convinced they needed schooling, by me if no-one better came along. That last tour of India was valedictory though I didn't know it at the time: ever since I've been hearing only of deaths, my dad and mum's generation falling to old age and illness, my cousins and contemporaries falling to pressure, expectations, alcoholism and madness. My own madness as the 80s close out and I ready myself for the outside world is that white people will never understand me, and that's proven a madness unbroken even now after all this bleeding chipping away through the medium of record reviews. I never ever ever talk race with white folk cos within a minute I want to slap 'em, within a minute they're telling me that it's me who's a racist, within a minute I know even more fervently that I'm right, that most white folk have not a frigging clue about racism and what it means. OK, let me *talk* to you about that that unshaken opinion. Once you've stopped shaking, and once I've answered that call.

Chapter 4

The True Divine Painter

The call? My friend, he said he'd be over. Getting excited? I am.

OK, first of all for fucks sake relax, I can see you shifting in your seat. No-one's on trial here. Stop being so fearful of incriminating yourself. Stop thinking that race is a minefield and just accept that now and then we all get our legs blown off when the way we're made comes into contact with others. Relax and realise you'll never be healed from the wound that is your skin. Its colour controls your past and your present and your future. That is not a limitation. Too much nervousness with talk of race, the instantaneous denials and protestations that in particular accompany the white response, a mistaken impulse for atonement, a dealing with, a righting of wrongs, that puts fears of inadequacy and bristling resentment in EVERYONE's response. Just because I think you white folks have a bigger problem than us lot doesn't mean we can't talk, doesn't mean that I can't accuse you without you feeling like I also want to wield the executioners axe. The only 'punishment' here is perhaps a little tweak up in your self-awareness, perhaps a little change in the way you talk and the way your brain works to make you talk. *And of course, the deeper tweak in my own prejudices so I can stop talking about you as if you're not here.* Astonishing how after so many years white folk can't realise how their bleating about what words they can/can't use, whining about what flags they can/can't fly, make them sound like such spoiled little fucks in a world where the brown'n'black are still at the bottom in every substantive sense. Can't talk race and pop because too many people think they're in the shackles or being given the slave masters' whip, that every word is gonna get pounced on. Anxiety of accusation means that we can't all acknowledge that racism isn't some single-issue habit that can be avoided or ejected but part of each and every one of us, not someone else's 'problem' but in ALL of our souls and thus a part of all of our responses to music. So, first, as if it's possible, relax, it's the best way to stay vigilant. It's nearly morning again. We'll be done with each other soon, I just want to point out that racism isn't just a problem for Western music, it's something that threatens to defile *any* music wherever racists see a chance. Listen to any Bismillah Khan, perhaps the single most inspirational musical artist of the 20th century this side of Miles Davis, and remind yourself how little any of us know, how much any of us can feel, how little caste and creed and colour can matter, how much they can matter.

"Is there no joy in music – is it all to be this foolishness? Money is nonsense. So long as the shehnai is with me, what need do I have for anything else? Musicians should be heard and not seen. See this shehnai? This is such a thing that when I lift it, I start thinking from my heart"

Born in 1916 in Bihar into a family of court musicians, Bismillah Khan was trained in the art of playing the shehnai, a small oboe/recorder style reed instrument that in Khan's hands could summon up eternity. More than anyone else, Khan helped bring what was essentially a folk instrument into the more formalised world of classical raga. A devout Shia Muslim, he was curiously also a staunch devotee of Saraswati, the Hindu goddess of music. His music and his religion were a divine unity. He lived in Benares and eschewed much of the wealth and trappings of success, picked up innumerable state honours, and spent his life making heaven in sound. Were I an expert, I could explain how Khan's meld of drone, tetrachord and powerful ornamentation combine to make magic. But I didn't learn this music; rather, it came to claim me. My dad would listen to him and it percolated through. When I'd take him a beer in the room with the stereo in it, I'd see him nearly in tears. Ever hungry for drone, I stole my dad's tapes and jammed along with a cracked Les Paul. After my dad died, I inherited the vinyl – beautiful records pressed up by the Gramophone Company Of India, mainly from the Sixties – and listened even closer and the tears began to flow seemingly from my dad through Khan's music and out of my own eyes. I realised that precisely the fucked-up beats, vocal freedom and anti-melodies I was digging in early Seventies Miles and Tim Buckley and drum'n'bass were being lashed down by these guys in the Twenties, never mind being played by innumerable genii since raga's inception in the 3rd Century BC. But it was Bismillah's glorious pipe-borne voice, Bismillah's soul that he spilled out through his shehnai (I own a shehnai, and can't even get a squeak out of it, let alone spend the two hours it takes Khan to tune the thing up), that perhaps first pulled me back in the late 90s to a fragile sense of belonging in Indian music. Within – on the plastic, in the grooves– were revolving doors to nebulae, trapdoors into galaxies, and turnstiles into a seemingly infinitesimal self-awareness. There's a peace to be found in Khan's music, but there's also anger, a celestial fury, the darkest blues and the bloodiest reds and the most tranquil yellows. It's an alternate universe where emotion finds clear expression and the sculpting of sound enfolds you. There's a soul-shaking humanity to his music, and that's maybe the most brave and beautiful thing about the maestro's undying art - the balance between restraint and abandon, surprise and fulfilment, and the sheer joyful melodic invention are inspirational, no matter what music you're into. Find any of the albums he did with the incredible violin player VG Jog, especially the Ragamala series of 'Morning To Midnight' ragas, and get yourself blessed by them, soon as. Because only beauty can save us now. And only tears can wash us new. And like all truly universal music, Kahn's sounds come from the tiny confines of his heart but illuminate anyone who dares step into their light. Kahn knew how music could be twisted for other ends, gently set in motion his music as glorious antidote to the perversion of sound for merely political intent. A muslim, who prayed to Hindu gods, played Hindu songs, an immortal embodiment of musical and spiritual freedom that in the mid-90s reminds me to be wary when music wears a flag, or even worse, a faith on its sleeve.

We've all of us, especially us British folk, got to be asking what it means to be one of us, be on the lookout for where that meaning hardens, and thickens. And we should all be aware of those frequent moments where music, a thing made of love, is used to shore up senses of national identity, simpler times, golden ages. As an Anglo-Indian (and Christ, how much do I have to suppress my gag-reflex when summating myself thus) who's spent much of my life out-Englishing the English, I'm paranoiacly aware, through a need to know my potential enemies, of what it can mean when white pop looks back wistfully. By the 90s, Britpop gave me plenty of reasons to be suspect, to wonder what dreams were getting re-animated when people harked back. Yeah 67/68 can mean revolution, but it can mean the Immigration Act the Labour Govt. bought in, it's neutering of Enoch's 67 campaigns, it's making of me as 'non-patrial', the grisly term of denial the act designated me and my folks. The letters I got from readers at the Melody Maker told me stuff – mainly that a lot of people were even wondering what the fuck I was doing writing for white music papers. Take my "black hip-hop shit elsewhere" was the most memorable advice, whilst their favourite bands draped themselves in the flag – I'll leave it to you to care whether I cared but I was nurturing my own guilty revisionism too. Whilst Oasis were finally and fatally winning Britishness back for the non-fey and charmless for good, I'm trapped and tripped out and looking back, and hiding in my own vintage duds as well, listening to tapes in a CD age, trying to look like I've just stepped off a boat (i.e. smart and sharp). And my own tone of nostalgia for Marathi film-song finds ugly compassion in the 90s & 00s on the city streets and villages of Maharashtra. Mumbai, like Coventry, is a place where you have to work fucking hard to be a racist; you're raised in a chaotic cosmopolitan fog of accents and languages – but in the past 20 years Mumbai, at its best is a model of daily natural religious tolerance, has been twisted by the equally idiotic manoeuvres of gunmen in hotels and the Shiv Sena. These self-proclaimed 'Army Of Sivaji' spread mayhem and fascist violence, spark anti-union riots and race-hate against Muslims and immigrant workers from other states, under the guise of *bhumiputr* ('native pride'), declaring only Marathi Hindus as true 'sons of the soil'. Their lunatic founder-leader, ex-cartoonist Balasaheb Thackeray, has spent his entire fetid Hitler-modelled political career spewing hatred of Islam and migrants to Maharashtra, calling for Hindu suicide squads to counteract 'Muslim violence', & only for "Marathi songs to be played on the radio". And the ironies like a stink rose unfold - Shivaji used as a figurehead of hatred, the guy whose bronze bust I proudly polish on my mantel, a warrior-king smart enough to know that religious tolerance was the key to uniting the people because the people practised religious tolerance naturally.

'Verily, Islam and Hinduism are terms of contrast. They are used by the true Divine Painter for blending the colours and filling in the outlines' - Shivaji Bhosle

Lata Mangeshkar, like all Marathi singers, sang songs about Shivaji because he was a hero to Marathis. In fact, she sang songs to him at the formation of the Maharashtran State, May 1st 1960 in Shivaji Park, Bombay. 50 years later in 2010, Lata, now convinced and close to the Thackeray's, sings in Bandra park Mumbai for Shiv Sena, at a celebration of Maharashtra's Golden Jubilee. Also in 2010, Asha Bhosle, Lata's sister, keeps the tension in their prickly relationship going by publicly declaring in Pune, now a Shiv Sena stronghold, that 'India is for all Indians, [regardless of religion]', much to the disgust of the Thackeray clan. Asha & Lata of course have history, a juicy half-century of fractiousness now legendary, but that starts in humble surroundings that hugely remind me of my own parents. Born, like my folks, into a large \Brahmin family in a tiny Maharashtrian hamlet (also including their lil composer-bro Hridaynath & lil' Sis & singer Usha who both also ended up making huge contributions to the explosion in Marathi film), the sisters are inseparably close at childhood. Lata drops out of school when told she can't tote her little sister along. As with my parents, Bombay eventually called the musical Mangeshkars out of the jungle. Upon the death of their theatre-actor father Asha & Lata moved to Bombay and quickly found themselves singing for the growing movie industry to support the family. A common move to the big smoke - with everyone born in such circum-stances in the 30s, Bombay is the city in which dreams of education or artistry or fame find themselves walking or washed up, and once roots are laid down, a flat found, a floor to sleep on, an understanding auntie or uncle, that city takes these people over, becomes their internal geography, becomes the place where they make it or fail. Lata and Asha would take trains and trams around Bombay, clutching umbrellas to auditions, frequently rejected as 'too thin' in vocal tone, in a fledgling movie-era where composers and songwriters always aimed for the loudly flamboyant. Lata made her Maharashtrian film-debut aged 14 in 1943, Asha in the same year aged 10. At age 16, Asha elopes with the 31-year-old Ganpatrao Bhosle, Lata's personal secretary, against Lata & her family's wishes. "It was a love marriage and Lata didi did not speak to me for a long time. She disapproved of the alliance." admitted Asha. Long-periods of total non-commu-nication between these previously intimate sisters have charac-terised their relationship ever since. A miserable marriage filled with mistreatment, Asha is thrown out by Bhosle in 1960, pregnant with her 3rd child, still singing for money, looking on as a raging, unforgiving and lovelorn Lata ascends to stardom. As the girls mother, Mai Mangeshkar said: "The more Lata suffered, the more her art excelled."

Certainly, there is something immutably astonishing about Lata's voice, something pure, something undeniable, something instant and miraculous, something that transcends time and language and messed up this little Indian boy even though I frequently had no idea what she was singing about (in fact got annoyed when my mum or dad tried in vain to explain it). No less an authority than classical music titan Ustad Amir Khan said: "What we classical musicians take 3 and 1/2 hours to accomplish, Lata does in 3 minutes." Crucially, it was Lata's playback singing that transformed Bollywood song, that freed up composers and directors to extend their compositions not only beyond what an actress or actor could manage, but beyond what most professional singers could achieve. In the early days of Marathi film the throaty, shouty nature of actor's singing-voices were matched by one-note, simplistic compositions – Lata opened that all up, gave composers a way-wider palette to play with, with her softer, more translucent tones, a means whereby subtlety and suggestion could find their way in. Veteran Bengali movie-star Kanan Devi summed it up: "Before the advent of playback singing the songs that we actresses sang were songs only in name. It is only after Lata started giving playback, that real music happened." And Anil Biswas, the pioneer of Bollywood playback-soundtracks and the first Indian composer to really introduce full-blooded orchestration into Indian film also admitted that ". . . Lata was a Godsend to us composers because with her around there was absolutely no limitations placed on our range. Such was her vocal artistry that we could explore the most complex reaches of compositions in the knowledge and confidence and that she could take it all in her stride." At the top of her game by the early 60s, and in a position of musical-godhead she's never let slip since, still Asha's relationships continue to infuriate Lata as the 60s & 70s roll on, especially as Asha's second-fiddle status to Lata starts getting more complexly evened out. Asha's relationship with legendary composer/director O. P. Nayyar widened the rift between the two sisters to the point that Nayyar decided that he would never work with Lata again. Lata herself insisted that directors work with no other singers before she'd sign on for them. "Asha and Lata" Nayyar observed, "staying in opposite flats at Bombay's Peddar Road, had a common maidservant. Now this maidservant had merely to come and tell the younger sister that Lata had just recorded something wonderful for Asha to lose her vocal poise. Such was her Lata phobia that it took me some months to convince Asha that she had a voice individualistic enough to evolve a singing style all of her own." Asha: "I worked for years to create a voice and a style that was different from Lata, so that I could carve my own niche and not be banished to live in my sister's shadow." To this day, Asha for me remains the true star, able to damn the entirety of current Hindi movie music with divinely weighted quotes like "There is a distinct lack of efforts on the part of the singers, as a result of which the songs being rendered are *sans* tone and emotions." She's still a glamour puss where her sister is settling nicely into the role of elder-stateswoman. Their variance and totally different responses to Shiv Sena are revealing and I think, make Asha the clear winner of my heart , in a sense the real constant pure *musician* in all of this. And still the stink rose keeps unfolding. Last time my mum went back a few months back, she found herself apoplectic at just how many of our relatives seemed to think it was OK to engage in precisely the kind of Islamophobia Shiv Sena have smeared across the Maharashtrian body politic. (Shiv Sena are currently co-opting protests about a planned nuclear facility in Konkan, the precise area of Maharashtra that my mum's family comes from). Feels like they're pressing in close. In the 90s, just as I'm finding my identity, it's getting hijacked by cunts and thugs, and I'm meeting more narrow-minded English Marathis, later arrivals than my parents, whose politics cause massive late night arguments with my folks when they come to our house, idiots with idiot offspring who grass me up for popping out for a fag.

One of my most vivid memories of returning to India at age 10 was sitting in Heathrow, listening to kids who looked like us but with American accents. Me and my sister did what we've always done when confronted with kids who ostensibly have the same genes & upbringing as us – we freaked the fuck out. My parents definitely always wanted us to be aware of our roots, but they let us pursue that very much on our own reconnaissance, through our own reading and listening. When my mum and dad set up an organisation called Marathi Mitra Mandal in the mid 80s as an attempt to get Marathi-speakers and Maharashtrian people together across the UK we finally started meeting los of kids who should've been like us, but whose desire for life extended no further than their parents predictions and limitations, who eventually wanted to move back to India. These kids, born and bred here, still seemed like they're visiting, like composites of their parents intransigence and their own cowed acceptance of that. Our folks left us to our own explorations. One crazy horrific week one long summer holiday my mum (wanting rid of a bored boy for a week) with a startling foolishness and to my sobbing protest, assented to let me go with a boy I hated to an RSS Hindu boys-training camp, wherein we were drilled and taught karate and emerged with a frighteningly militaristic mindset that my friends were appalled to see had taken me over like a zombie-virus. My memories of this are hazy for several reasons. Firstly I've tried to blot it out. Secondly, the boy I went with was a twat and I have no desire to get in touch with him to recall the events. I just remember sleeping in what seemed like a school-hall in Leicester, woken at 6 by a whistle, horrible breakfast of rice pudding (no toast in the new Hindu nation), martial arts training for the unspecified reason of 'a Hindu needs to fight for his faith', some light work with weapons. I came out a fruitloop. It had only taken 7 days of harsh routine but for a while back there, I knew what it felt like to become a fascist, a nazi, an unthinking automaton convinced you're the only one thinking, a stormtrooper. What I did notice about the other boys there was that their folks had their whole lives planned before they even got to live them and it was encounters like this and my return to reality afterwards that ensured I have always felt alienated not just from England, but from any notion of a homeland, and any notion of a community within the frequently shitwitted racist Brahmin community. Once a game of footy in my back-garden had enabled me to return to my own natural abnormality, that week in that RSS camp and my immediate thoughts afterwards, coming back to reality, were close to madness, the feeling of being on a physical plateau of mechanical glee, then realising it's built on mental tricks and outright lies it takes a day to clamber down from. In truth, and scarily, it was a rather *weak* Midlands-version of the much-scarier khaki-shorted neo-fascist schools in India currently churning out fascist thugs by the bucketload – now it seems like a dream, a week in which though I'd not under-stood anything but had ended up believing every word of it. Quickly surmised anyhoo- fatherlands is for hatstands, brain-washed robots of their hateful parents creation. I now pity those boys dim enough for it to last within, even that twat I went with (my constant need for a fag during the week also militated against my total militarization somewhat). It was frequently those same parents, desperate to prove their 'loyalty' to their abandoned birthplace, who ended up having night-long arguments with my mum and dad, I'd lie awake hearing raised Marathi voices always on the same subject, nationalism, race, Islam & Hinduism. My dad would emerge from these shouting matches hoarse, appalled, initially cos of our youth insistent that me and my sister should be protected from his own communities' frightening ability for prejudice, later on letting us hear it in all its stupidity and venality. I've been hearing it & reading it from stuck-up, idiotic Maharashtrian Brahmins ever since.

Shiv Sena's rise is part of the reason I haven't been back in many years. Thackeray's project was to take on the Marathi-extremism of Savakar's Hindutva ideology and make it even more extreme, even more violent. Shiv Sena's own newsletter (called *Saamana* – 'Confrontation') is clearly inspired by Tilak's inflammatory tactics if not his secular politics. In it through the 80s & 90s Thackeray vomits up his race-hate, his religious hate , his immigrant-hate, calls Islam a 'cancer that must be operated on', criticises Sachin Tendulkar as a 'traitor' when he dares to publically state that he's 'a proud Maharastrian but an Indian first and foremost'. In 1992, when BJP & Shiv Sena thugs destroy the Babri Masjid mosque in Ajodhya, kicking off 2 days of riots that lead to a thousand Muslim deaths he's unrepentant, starts being known as 'remote control' cos of the power his extremism exerts over policy-decisions and rhetoric in mainstream governance.

But when Sena try and wage cultural wars in Maharastra, and attempt to protect Mumbai from immigrant influence, they always run into trouble, ill-equipped as their rhetoric is to deal with culture's slipperiness in India, or the tolerant realities of Mumbai life where in truth only about 28% of the population are Marathi. Mumbai's history is not of purity - not even of being a 'Marathi' stronghold until Thackray's father Prabodhankar, alongside his fellow dipshits in the Samyukta Maharashtra Samiti movement that pushed for Marathi independence in the 50s, start creating this entirely erroneous picture of Mumbai as ancient Maratha stronghold. As 'Bombay' Mumbai was a string of islands first held by the Portugese until the mid 17th century, then the British. Shivaji never developed Mumbai as his base, preferring Raigad in Konkan. The Maratha empire's expansion in the 18th century came culturally & politically from Pune and the Peshwas Sivaji had established there, not Mumbai at all. Sena's attempted 'Mumbai-isation' of the Marathi identity is perceived by many to be the cause of the decline in Marathi culture, far more damaging than the constant influx of immigrants that has been Mumbais lifeblood since its beginnings. Sena's paranoid focus on Mumbai as stronghold has marginalised those places like Pune, Kolhapur & Satara that were traditional places of Marathi scholarship. The diversity of local theatre, art and poetry, and the cinema that reflected an indigenous Marathi ethos has been swallowed whole by Mumbai's purely mercenary cultural instincts. Sena's rise as a state-backed, anti-working class force of thugs has effectively snuffed out centres of living Marathi culture like Girangaon, the area my family first lived in in Mumbai & one in which they still do, a once proud working-class neighbourhood now decimated by the hostility of Sena's cretinous mobs. Even though Bal Thackeray's caste, like many high-castes except for Chitpavan Bhramins, was actually pro-British during the Raj, him and his brothers now rail against North Indian cinema such as Bhojpuri films as corrupting a pure Hindutva Maharashtrian culture. Thackeray's brothers are caricatures of Bal, just as he himself is a fascist caricature of the humanist Marathi cultural leaders who came from places like Girangaon. It is as yet unclear as to whether Shiv Sena's star is still on the rise, or beginning a swandive into the footnotes of history.

Thackeray, Shiv Sena & the BJP's use of Marathi music to perpetuate their rot is almost enough to make me stick all my old Marathi vinyl and tapes up in the attic to wait for a calmer age. Of course, the lies of Thackeray are why I never can do that. Music's mis-use by racists and racist nations particularly irks because it's an exploitation of an artform that survives because it's communication between times and places and contains the history of ALL the people who pass it on that journey. Marathi music whether classical, folk or cinematic is always absolutely dependent, as is all Indian music, on the influence of Islam, and the intransigent eternity of ancient Vedic music, and the way those two forces do the do, get busy, get down and get funky with it - drone derailed, melody endless and triumphant. Listening, as my dad did nigh-on incessantly to another genius of Indian classical music, Bhimsen Joshi, what you can hear, through his cracked alcohol-drenched voice, is the sound of Sena-style prejudice blasted apart.

Born in the State that borders Maharashtra to the south, Karnataka, Joshi actually grew up in the care of his parents & grandparents in a Kulkarni household, the Brahmin-home of the village scribes. A strangely unbending, stubborn child, Joshi was in a constant state of running-away-from-home, once legging it to the wild yonder for the simple reason that his mum wouldn't give him a second-spoonful of ghee with his dinner. Music pulled and entranced him from a young age, he stole a Tanpura that'd been hidden from him by his school-teacher dad who had an engineers-future planned for him, and frequently absconded from the family's room altogether to locate sounds, whether a passing bhajan singing procession or an azaan from the nearby mosque. Like so many of us since though, it was a recording that first made the young Joshi think about music as not just a fascination but a way of life: a scratchy 78 of Abdul Karim Khan's Thumri *"Piya Bin Nahi Aavat Chain"* was enough for Joshi to leave his home in 1933, 11-years-old and hungry to find a master and learn music. Sleeping on Bombay railway platforms, eating leftovers, with the help of money lent by his co-passengers in the train Bhimsen reached Dharwad first and later went to Pune. Later he moved to Gwalior and got into the prestigious Madhava Music School, a *gharana* or music-community under the tutelage of the famous sarod player Hafiz Ali Khan. Wanderlust, and the need for new sounds had him then travelling for three years around North India trying to find a good guru, passing out in-front of mosques out of sheer starvation, kicked awake hearing ghazal, before his dad could track him down and drag him home. In 36, legendary Marathi actor Rambhau Kundgolkar, a native of Dharwad, agreed to be his guru. Joshi stayed at his house in the traditional guru-shishya (teacher-student) tradition, gleaning knowledge of music from his master as and when he could, while performing odd-jobs in his house till 1940. By then, the 18-yr old Joshi was ready to take on the world and the cosmos: playing live in '41 got him a record deal by '42 and by '43 he was in Bombay, a radio star, hailed by critics, loved by crowds. Part of the reason for that acclaim was down to Joshi's restless spirit: it was clear to anyone who heard him that here was a musician who'd steeped himself in all kinds of different traditions and memories, a musician who was ever the wanderer, engendering brilliant phrases more intuitively than through deliberation, mixing the cerebral, austere, sensual and spiritual whenever he stepped to a mic, proof in sound that music thrives on the half-caste, the mixed-up, the human heart more than the human religion, or the human nation.

Missionary, evangelical Abrahamanic faiths whether Mughal or British have always run into the same problem with India. The vastness and variety of unscripted, unbroken spiritual practice, local but linked, was always finally impervious to books, the written word of god. The smartest invaders soon realised that giving India architecture and infrastructure could impose a control stronger than the superimposition (for that is all it ever could be) of a foreign faith. Akbar knew it, and so Shivaji followed - people meet and play together, can't be stopped. And so in the middle of the last millennium, Sufi mystics and Sultanate courts bring new tunes, new instruments, new forms like ghazal and qawwalli. As ever, music's potential for abstraction gives it a generosity - a universality too slippery for politics' dull manoeuvres, too powerful a slipstream to not careen over those divides, only existing when flowing on beyond petty man-made notions like race, nation or state, living irrefutable proof that Shiv Sena's project is a contemptibly ignorant, anti-artistic battle cry of inhumanity. Why else would an Islamic shehnai master like Ustad Bismillah Khan be most famous for playing *Raghu Pati Raghav Raja Ram*, a tune I vividly remember my mum and dad singing at the temple in the morning, an ageless ancient tune ostensibly Hindu but as memory-burned by the desert and the mountain range as it is by the jungle and the river? And the city's own new seething. One of Gandhi's favourites, another old Indian who knew how precarious notions of Indian identity could be when shot through with bigotry or fear, the way wilful historical ignorance so often ignores the ways people really are, preys on resentment to turn natural respect and love into a deviant enmity ("To think that I should be dubbed an enemy to an art like music because I favour asceticism! I, who cannot even conceive of the evolution of India's religious life without her music!"). Throughout Bhimsen Joshi's work, that ancient history of cross-pollination and bastardised intrigue is bought to its soulful zenith. Listening to him, you hear a man pushing his voice and himself to the limit, actually thriving on that razor's edge where you have to admit you're seeking something entirely unattainable. In Joshi's work, the lies of Shiv Sena are destroyed in a breath, obliterated in a moment.

It's simply not possible, let alone desirable, to listen to Indian classical music, such a huge part of Maharashtra's pre-cinematic & Bollywood-cinematic musical history, without hearing Islam's influence. Shivaji himself as Emperor of the Marathas, declaring independence from Muslim rule, was clever enough to realise that it's the secular state that endures, and it's in the 17th century, when Shivaji's empire sought to emulate the tolerance and open-mindedness of Muslim sultanates around India, that Maharashtrian music takes massive leaps ahead, absorbing hugely important lessons from Iran, schooling itself from the ghazal of Pashtuns from what's now Afghanistan and Pakistan (and back then was all Bharat, or India), from the Mughal-court musicians who bought their own traditions and instrumentation from as far afield as Eastern Europe and the Middle East. Indian classical music is a polyglot mess of this itinerant innovation and intrigue, so it's no accident that when Bhimsen Joshi died in January 2010, Shiv Sena made no attempt to pretend he was some voice from a faux-Hindutva past. Shiv Sena, like Balchandra Tilak, like Vinayak Damodar Savarkar and the BJP/RSS cretins who have followed him all hail back to Shivaji's Maratha empire, the last Indian empire before the invasion of the British, but they miss its tolerance, miss the fact it succeeded for 150 years by being open to older ideas from elsewhere. Politically, for all the progress the 20th century brings to India, there's also a lot of regression, revisionism. Pune, the city from which so much Chitpavan political subversion and resistance originated from, was only built into a city through the largesse of the Peshwa system, Peshwa itself a Mughal word meaning 'foremost'. The movie songs which celebrate Shivaji, which can still be tied in with a Marathi film-industry and a golden age concurrent (although still pre-dating) independence are utilisable by poltroons on the right – the ancient music that is the wellspring of those folk and film songs is less easy to crowbar into such modern rigidity. When I first heard Joshi I pissed myself. His voice made me laugh - it may well do the same for you, possibly because like me you've grown up thinking that voices can only do certain things, that someone like Tim Buckley is the limit of what the throat can do. Stay with Joshi and you'll find yourself breathless, wracked, hand on mouth to keep in the gasps. Listen to his rendition of *Raag Miyan Ki Todi*, or *Dadra In Raga Mishra Gara*, or his epic reading of *Raag Puriya Dhanashree* and you'll hear that his music, like all great Indian music, consistently defies the post-colonial partitions, the opportunistic games played by politicians with Indian 'identity'. His voice, when you hear it and let it take you, is an inexhaustible repos-

77

itory of human experience and emotion that absolutely breaks over such barriers like a tsunami, that reveals exactly how much he learned from the Muslim pioneers of modern vocal-Raga and Kyall (Abdul Karim Khan and Abdul Wahid Khan), how he was astonishing precisely because his music destroys even the confines of his *Gharana* (perhaps the last lesson of the *Gharana*) and springs from the faithless wonder, and sacred fearlessness that has characterised Indian music for thousands of years. Muslims and Hindus have sung in each others temples and mosques for a millennium - Joshi's music is proof that Raga is simply a framework within which anything can happen, his melodies the most astonishing modernist improvisations within that ancient framework, his songs as Islamic as they are heathen, as prehistoric as they are futuristic, as civilized as they are untamed. The honest rawness you can hear in a Joshi recording is down to the humility and no-bullshit conviction of the man himself. When people would applaud a particularly dazzling vocal run, he'd grab the mic: "clap after it's all over". As his health failed him he'd simply stop mid-concert: "Can you stick a plucked flower to the plant and expect it to blossom?! No, I can't continue any more...".

What I learned in the 80s and 90s, digging deep into the concepts behind Indian music, is that those strictures - *raga, swara, shruti, alankar, taal* - you might read as confinements are there to be broken and blended and played with, that music only progresses when the societies that musicians come from are invaded, overthrown, absorbed, kidnapped, emancipated, returned palpably and audibly changed. It's something that's encoded into the very structures of Indian classical-music learning itself. A *gharana* is a fuzzy, secret concept, impervious to outside interrogation: the only insight you can gain into its closed-doors are when its students emerge and start singing – less a conventional school or academy, more a system of social organization linking musicians or dancers by lineage and/or apprenticeship, and by adherence to a particular musical style. It's a school, unlike my own, (and perhaps unlike the Western stageschool models that seem to be churning out the shite drowning us all right now) that thrives on multiformity, on teaching and learning advancing to the point where they are one. What you can tell when you hear the work of Joshi, or Ustad Abdul Karim Kahn or Ghulam Ali Kahn is that what went on in these places wasn't simply the passing on of a tradition. It was the exploration of resonances, of the lexicon of music and how it related to grammatical structures, conceptual patterns and modes of imagination and expression fed in from diverse individuals and the rich traditions they belonged to. That diversity is key, Bhimsen Joshi was nurtured and shaped by a musical culture that had multiple traditions so what emerged was entirely heterogeneous, a rigorous training that through oral transmission incorporated both living and non-living voices, that then encouraged experimentation with that voice freshly found, the sharing of experiences to push music beyond the merely sterile intellectual framework you might imagine when you read about the daunting esoteric concepts behind *raag*.

Immigration of people and ideas is the lifeblood of music - has been since time immemorial - and when you hear Joshi, there can be no doubt. You hear that, yes, vocal chords and lungs and minds and imaginations can be trained within a society to do things that are superhuman, but they can only resonate within you still, can only attain true immortality, when tied to a heart open to all human experience, all human lives, all human music. Indian classical music is so often talked about as a system and that implies strictures and in the west, strictures imply impris- onment - a blueprint whose confinements and limitations you can't stray beyond, something to resist like any good romantic. But in contrast to the pointless piddling-about that Western models of musical-freedom so often inspire, the discipline and intense intent of Eastern music is peopled by artists who can't help but use the confines of their training to explore the infinite: these aren't people who see being a musician as essentially pissing about prettily, but people for whom music is the only discipline in their life. And crucially, that discipline can be appreciated when listening, but can be ignored – and then you're in a firestorm of the soul, the endless sound of a heart's supernova. Ragas are meant to be played at certain times of the day but how right do they sound at 2.am when nothing else makes sense? Joshi was a raging alcoholic but even in his later recordings and especially on his stunning film-soundtrack work with Lata, you can hear an artist absolutely committed - spiritually, intellectually and musically - to exploring all the possibilities, pushing the boundaries to unlock the infinity of expression and precision that the raga mode affords it's most expert proponents. Lack of notation is key - oral transmission as opposed to the tyranny of text opens up the possibility of whispers going awry, of learning being challenged before it can turn into orthodoxy, of sounds mutating through race, religion, and in the white-hot inferno that forges the two in the heart. Every time I hear Joshi I hear something new. It's because Indian classical music isn't a system. It's a launch pad into infinite space, whether that's cosmic or metaphysical, emotional or intellectual.

Perhaps it's that daunting rigor of Indian classical music that's made its absorption in the West so cosmetic and piecemeal, the mistaken idea that simply by copping the instrumentation you're taking on the culture, the fkn Nehru-jacketed hippy-move of sticking a sitar where a guitar would've been. The only western musician I think to genuinely try and take on the structural as opposed to superficial oddity of this music is Miles Davis. 'On The Corner' is perhaps a dilletante's treatment, layered with sitar & tabla, but by the time he's making pieces like 'He Loved Him Madly' & 'Mtume' you can hear the same sense of repetition as both hypnosis & scarifier, the same impossibly huge mathematical structures coming across as pure improvisational heat, perhaps only possible with Western modes of playing if you've got a genius like Teo Macero on the cut. Beyond Miles' omnivourous omnipotent genius though this stuff is mis-used everywhere. If musicians can't get a handle on it, I guess we shouldn't be surprised that it suits racist scumfucks like Shiv Sena to fundamentally misunderstand music, to bound it to an earth they see in terms of fear and loathing and lines between us. By the 90s, I was realising that the attempt to either assert a false racial history, or worse (because a dishonest liberal move) pretend that race has *no* part to play in music, were two sides of the same ignorant-assed coin. It both denies music its real significance and runs scared of confronting those moments when music is given new uglier significances. The difference being that by the 90s I was writing about it. I remember, it took me three reviews to figure out what it was I wanted to say and I've been banging on about it ever since. Don't be daft, you're not going to start me making sense now: the English stain I am cannot be bleached out, even if what I have to say is nearly done, even if I'm minded at my age to let it go, leave it, let it go, leave it, hide out with my fam for the next 50 years and let the natural destruction of race-as-monolith take a few generations of fucking and making gorgeous little mixed-race babies to finally kick in. Before the dawn, I want to break down your pedigree to find out mine. You've got to stay awake and witness. I want both us mongrels to meet.

Chapter 5

Worms In A Fig

Sure, keep building and burning, we're here all night A decade ago, another Thursday night, two days after the twin towers fall I'm walking home from band practice, blissfully sated, crossing a junction, aware of some pointing and jostling of elbows in the boy-racer to my left. Engine revs as I cross, laughter. Older fears than the lads in the car rise up inside. Make it to the kerb, ambler gamblers off down the ave., a half-second of relieved silent self-mocking, then some real loud mocking out the wound-down window. The word shouted from shotgun is loud and greeted by much back-seat guffawing. The word is "bomber".

Now where should the camera go, whose story warrants chasing? The doddery old twat on the side of the kerb thinking 'what?' Nahh, course not, follow the hate, follow the haters, the 'questions' they ask. Always deal with the 'issue', the 'problem' of us being here, the gift of your tolerance our only redemption. Those lads probably forgot about that high-larious moment pretty quick. A decade on I haven't. You never do, you keep every single moment like that locked in raw, to be returned to and prodded to feel the hit, an endlessly renewable graze on your future. Public moments, riots, cases such as Stephen Lawrence, leave similar raw scars because beyond the pity the press feel, you feel an instant compassion because you've been in similarly charged, terrifying situations of standing tall feeling small. I can let the lenses follow those boy racers cos I've had cameras swooping around me my whole life, as a way of dealing with routine, and as a way of dealing with moments when you're young and you see your kind attacked, abused, laughed at, on streets and on the screens you hide in to avoid the streets awhile, and you're too young, and too scared, to step in and change things. It confuses you, angers you, fucks you up, and at a young age can turn you a bit stroppy and inward, never leaves. And because it happens for my ol' generation at a young age, it's important. It'll keep happening (at the moment, increasingly) and even though at my age now you greet that with a shrug rather than a snarl – the odd street-level bit of outright abuse, the trains and pubs you still avoid. It's part of you like your astronaut name, a problem unless you can stop thinking of *their* route here and start breaking down your own pedigree, skewering that tendency when it comes to the 'Asian' experience of Asians more than willing to make the whole thing into a gag, a comic series of embarrassments and cultural misunder-standings, white folk willing to be amused by Asian experience so long as it never tries to be any more than a vignette, whilst also indulging a titillated liberal excitement about those moments when white style-culture bleeds into pure out'n'proud racism.

When I say 'white style culture' I mean really, white working class culture as reimagined by middle-class white culture, and for the past 2 decades that seems to be all that I've been presented with whether it's current fears about blackenized white 'gangs', or hipper fascinations with white-power politics. The working class, so often characterised by the liberal wittering-classes as those people 'prone' to racism, 'prone' to the propa-ganda of the NF or BNP, are actually the pakis of the British class system, talked about as if they're not there, fair game for whatever blowhard wants to spin their panaceas & restoratives to sick Britain, as if working-class Britain is a simpler-celled Petri-dish wherein the middle-classes can foresee a future to fear. And that cultural smugness equates to both wrong-headed condemnations and mealy-mouthed excuses: so often in discussion of how racism is rearing it's head again (like it's ever been away) in the 'sink-estates' & the white-ghettos of our cities and coasts there's the idea perpetuated that by being *working-class* supporters of crypto-fascist parties people are somehow excused from being called the racist cunts they are (it's the white working class who live alongside them who have the balls to call them racist cunts, not the fucking politicians). Uncannily mirrors the condescension that ethnic minorities get – secretly suggests that racist Britons have a mainline to a truth, instinctiveness, honesty and 'soul' the politician and the journalist and the bureaucrat will never get, that authority always needs to talk to and contain those concerns about immigration, those 'concerns' that need to be 'addressed' through an ever-harsher treatment of immigrants, rather than confronted in the hearts of the natives. The subtle deeper lie here, uncannily like that experienced by the immigrant population, is that the working class experience is one that isn't actually open to interpretation by the people living it, can only be objectively 'dealt with' by those lucky enough to be viewing it from above. The condescension & hypocrisy of talking about racist estates when the BNP have always been more electorally embedded in middle-class neighbourhoods shows how readily that class sublimates it's own bigotry downward, the creation of a racial war in the desperate attempt to avoid the real war between haves and have-nots. Immigration is always a 'battle-ground' for the haves. A frontline manned with those dashed poor tracksuit-wearing blighters who have to live next door to these ululating darkies. Those poor poor blighters, they know the score that's why they hate jonnyforeigner so much, lets turn our perceptions of that 'hate' into every other front page, every other policy document, every other speech at every other rally and remember – john bull can't ever play roles, switch, be as schizo-phrenic and playful and free as the next patient in this shock corridor called England, he's too busy belonging to the Great British Public. That self-exonerating condescencion infects deep, from journalism to art in the uk, the columns to the mini-series to the movies to the music - inevitably given that most UK pop right now seems to be made by a pack of chortling Britschool-alumni and kids-with-famous-dads who all shopped at the same fkn vegan-delicatessen through the noughties, a banishment/ vanishment of class from pop that enables the middle-classes who run the industry to choke all other voices out of existence. No-one in pop will admit it but unless you're listening to the most underground grime, bashment or hip-hop your musical intake is almost entirely middle class, and thus unsurprisingly superficial and retrograde, in the UK now. UK indie-rock for the past 20 years has been owned by the kind of self-avowed lads who think that by calling everything 'proper', 'class', 'top' and 'quality' and walking like a monkey they're somehow closer to the real life as lived 'on the streets', seemingly utterly unaware that to really survive on the streets you have to find a way to levitate, rise above, disappear, make your imagination a big enough place to live in. These people have small imaginations cos they've never had to grow a bigger one, never had to save their life and remake it.

For most of Britain's spotlit creatives and music-makers (because now being those things no longer means being politically aware – i.e. something you can't fucking learn at stage-school) there's a self-congratulatory backslap that race, and class, has 'sorted itself out' in the UK. It's the only reason I can think as to why British pop music hasn't said a fucking single thing of any import in such a long time. If race is mentioned by whitefolk it's in a flight to the extremes for security – the endless 'shock' at the EDL, the never-ending obsession with Skinhead culture as shown in 'This Is England' or Gavin Watson's 'Skins' - the post-hardmod Brit-lad mindset that by engrossing yourself in the extreme-edges of white-solidarity you're somehow going through the fire, realising what it is to be British. More often than not in these 'artistic looks' I find a surreptitious pleasure, a yearning for broken-times long gone. That yearning goes deep into indie rock as I become a pop writer, even if I ended up as a writer at a paper that nurtured & encouraged my fucked-offness. It was a great training which means that I could never belong the way writers belong to the music-scene now, because alternative/independent culture as I grow up, becomes less and less about 'boring old politics', less about trying to reinvoke genuinely lost aspects of Englishness to point to a new future, and more and more an exercise in obvious canonical nostalgia, particularly the kind that drapes itself in the union jack and that gets written about by writers who want to be on telly, the kind of nostalgia only interested in the erosion of ambivalence and the shoring up of an essentially imperialist Englishness that seeks to shut me out, fantasises easier times when our migration to your land was less visible, more 'controlled', more fearful. 'Alternative' culture has got stronger and stronger through this painfully shrunken idea of what it is to be English. My love for it has grown weaker and weaker as a result.

Of course, the cheques, infrequent and impossibly difficult to obtain, were much appreciated, the terminal and fatal retrospect of UK indie-pop has given me plenty of hatchet work over the years but truthfully, I'm more disappointed than angry, more heartbroken by a clear creativity that sought to exclude me. At a young young age, back when I'm naïve enough to think that racism is about skin-colour, I seek out the freaks for friends, the Goths and indie-kids and queers and metal kids whose playlists mirror my own and who's superficial appearance marks them out for ridicule and loathing from the mainstream. Only later do I realise that whilst some of them understand me as I understand them, those subcultures and societies and sexualities have their own reactionary enclaves. The Smiths are at the root of my queasy relationship with the music that should've been my home (I was a speccy wordy spotty little ponce – how could I not have been an indie kid?). I loved them, passionately, for 2 singles. The rot set in that infatuation as I heard and read deeper. By the time

I knew that Morrissey hated rap, black pop and "dislikes Pakistanis immensely", by the time of 'Asian Rut' and 'Bengali In Platforms' and 'National Front Disco', I knew that his dreams didn't include me, that me and my kind were a problem, an(other) obstacle in his vision of English pop progress/regress. There's something about The Smiths that still has an unhealthy hold over people you'd love to love, still has an unhealthy hold over me because compared to a modern guitar-pop that simply avoids politics or Englishness apart from in the smug observational agglomeration of clichés, buzzwords & trending-phrases, The Smiths were about what it truly is to be British, about nostalgia, about destroying any black trace in pop, pretty much a rights-for-whites insistence that nothing since punk had mattered. Even beyond the 60s love of Marr's shimmer and spray, Morrissey seemed to be harking back even further, back to the 50s, back to a time when rock'n'rollers could be counted upon by Moseley to spark mayhem in 58 - Morrissey, though clearly to me a Ted-fixated pre-immigration-fantasising Granny of a man, was perhaps the only British front man to really reveal what being British and white meant, what history is getting re-enacted when a British white front-man steps to the mic and can only look back in horror at the present. Even though he laid the groundwork of morose retrospect that lad-rock would later find its spiritual motivation, I can't join in convincingly now with the pack that pounces whenever the dumb old queen opens his mouth. For Moz to get dissed for nostalgia and fear by that shitrag the NME would be funny if it weren't so grisly to watch.– the Peter Pan of Weltschmerz with his rotating monomania & myopia gives me an honesty about his little Englander mindset that I actually come to prefer over the cowardly political silence of his descendants, although I listen to the music of neither. The injured regret, the post-colonial revulsion of Morrissey's music is closer to white England's heartbeat than anyone else will admit to being. I've got letter bombs to send and trains to derail and the great cleansing to plan so I don't listen to the Smiths any more but I know they're there, I know what lines they define for themselves and for me, how their underlying message – that black pop, if it's to be used, was better back when black folk knew their place (i.e. Jim Crow America in the early 60s) – started prevailing so much with lad-rock's ascendancy in the 90s, and still prevails. I also know why, say, other retrograde racially fantastical stuff like Gavin Watson's 'Skins' now gets called 'important', a 'cult classic'. When reissued in 2006 the vacuous twats over at Vice called it, "One of the best and most important books about youth fashion and culture ever published". For me that fetishisation of fascism those things like 'Skins' and 'This Is England' engage in reveal the grisly truth of white thinking about black culture. They wish it frozen, they wish it trapped, they wish it had all stopped long before black people got the damn-fool idea that they should be taken seriously, a constant wish that black music would fit into those historical categories that are still palatable and usable by white rock, whether that's reggae 'fans' who won't listen beyond the late 70s, or soul fans who won't listen beyond the mid 80s or hip-hop fans who won't listen beyond the 90s. It suits white narratives that Jamaica lost it's righteousness when it went electric, that soul music has become 'soulless', that hip-hop has 'lost it's way': it allows a lazy white culture not only to bemoan and prescribe black music's freedom, but also keeps these musics, that might threaten the white-rock hegemony, down to a closely curated cannon of classic texts. This is still a problem right fucking now – if anything it's getting worse, pop-crits digging the most obscurantist 3rd-world esoterica often merely as a handy way of deflecting any political criticism of their essentially Orientalist mindset before it can be expressed. Always be doubtful when the dominant musical culture repeatedly insists race 'isn't an issue' any more, you can be damn sure that merely means it's unspoken, it's seething, and those in charge are simply choosing to ignore it, pretend it doesn't matter when it matters more than ever. White bands used to listen to contemporary black music, be inspired and fired by it, had a natural ease in their relationship with black musicians (esp. the Stones, which is partly why they've always been my favourite band)– now they're more likely to pay it lip-service for the purposes of emphasising their own eclecticism, whilst tacitly perpetuating the comforting notion that the really important moves in music are always made by thoughtful polymaths like themselves, not the hardened more unsparing cultures that they thieve from. Notice how only the white underground is worthy of consideration or celebration by the mainstream. The black underground has to scrub itself clean, or plunge into full-blown tittilation (Odd Future) to even be heard by the mainstream anymore. It's what happens when the middle-classes colonise pop-talk, colonise pop – you get people more able to tart up their ignorance of new black art (alongside a hipster-glee in the most moneyed-up & shackled emanations from the white-owned black cultural mainstream), as merely a matter of taste & aesthetics, rather than the entirely revealing political choice their ignorance implies. And if a culture like indie can't help but yearn in its clothes and its looks and its sound for a time when black folk were excluded and powerless, when black music only exerted a hold on those 'cool' enough to know about it, fantasies of separatism, fantasies of simpler times when lines could be more clearly drawn become potent and persuasive. Critics at the moment are the fucking exemplifiers of this. There's a compulsion behind rockcrit to make black music step to a monolithic movement, a fixation on the manageable 'classic' era that kills the need for further investigation. The collector-mentality likes ticking off genres tokenistically, making sure their racks have the requisite amount of hip-hop, or reggae, or jazz or soul or grime in there to assuage any liberal guilt, but that then leaves it at that before the illiberal compelling heart of modern dancehall or hip-hop can confuse the order or integrity of the cannon. At the moment, as always, there's plenty of white folk standing round a hole in the ground flinging handfuls of dust over hip-hop's empty coffin, as ever, hip-hop itself stubbornly refuses to die or disappear so long as DJs keep spinning and MCs keep spitting: the infinite possibilities of the form are too enduring for it to just fizzle out merely cos the mainstream's being cowardly. But when hip-hop kills it, as it still does across the web across the wires and in the head, when it lashes down the spontaneous combustion that is its forte don't expect anyone with a word-count and a deadline to be listening, don't expect their fixations on the past to even allow them to dig hip-hop's endless parricidal progress into the future. Like the pencil-pushers who decried'n'derided Isaac Hayes as a purveyor of 'blacMuzakkk', insistent that r&b must never want more than the three-minute single, the production line, the tin-shack. Like the worst, most retro-fixated anti-mod-mods who think reggae 'degenerated' into dancehall, who stop listening to Jamaica as soon as *Heart Of The Congos* has stopped: those same people who even now haven't got an ear cocked Jamaica's way — damn foolish considering how often that tiny island has changed the world of sound. Pronouncing a music dead or washed up or 'in danger' is useful in covering up the reasons for that wilfully lazy ignorance, and the deeper racial reasons behind that music's continued marginalisation. Always the secret yearn for a simpler time, when white music dominated, a yearn that still exerts ultimate power over what we hear and what we get to hear. A nostalgia reflected in the convenient 'cleansing' an engrossment in white extremism affords it's liberal fans. Course we're not racist. THEY were racist. Back THEN.

Skins presents itself as documentary but it's pure fantasy, of better, stronger times for white identity. It presents people at the bottom of the ladder, who seemingly couldn't deal with change, but uses their obstinacy as both that which makes them heroic and supposedly that which separates them from the lovers of

Skins now – tease out that hipster politrickal slickness a little and you usually find a similar obstinacy in readings of black culture and music, a similarly luddite affection for black music's past and disappointment with black music's present (and those 'chavs' – is there a more pervasively damaging word in Britain right now? – who follow it). First printed in 1994, *Skins'* steely-eyed photographs of Watson's family and friends, tooling around Wycombe with nothing to do and everything to prove in the late Seventies and early Eighties, capture the moment when skin culture became a purely provincial form of resistance at the tail end of the Seventies: a barely coherent (yet talismanic and nostalgic) refusal of changing trends, and a reaffirmation of white working-class solidarity and rabblish resistance in the emerging Thatcher era. Wannabe hooligans and cultural studies lecturers will be equally tumescent but a couple of problems shoot out as soon as you start leafing through *Skins*. One – the photographs are, in the main forced, sentimentalised, unrevealing: clichéd portrayals in service to their subject's self-aggrandisement and self-pity, and seemingly bereft of insight or energy. There is shot after shot of skins looking hard, at odds with the world, facing down the lens with a smug mob-confidence that barely hints at the vulnerability beneath the tats and the chrome-domes. Sure, it's revealing of the political bubble skinhead culture willed itself into inhabiting, but the shots of skins sporting Skrewdriver T-shirts, scrawling NF graffiti and sieg-heiling down their local are too charged (and despite Watson's foreword protestations about it not being about race – knowingly so) to be presented as apolitical verité. Looking at the shots of this supposedly oppressed minority culture (that included blacks and whites lest we forget) I remember how the mere sight of a skinhead made me feel in the Seventies, how me and my family felt under physical threat whenever a Harrington and a crew cut hoved into view. You could say that it's the precise insularity of *Skins* that is revealing, that immerses you so

completely in their world – I'd say *Skins'* absolute refusal to deal
with the wider political realities of the world it depicts is a cop-
out, and the nostalgic back-pat it gives to a bunch of racist dicks
who made UK-Asian life just that little bit more terrifying in the
Seventies is too much for this Paki to stomach. For some, the
expanded reissue was a reminder of something sadly lost to our
pop culture. For someone who remembers the rise of the NF and
the battles of the early Eighties, it was merely a montage of
idiocy, aggression and race-hate enjoyable only as a tombstone to
a thankfully dead community of cunts and fascist scum who
found themselves unable to deal with a changing Britain. Prime
thug-porn wanking material for Morrissey, I'm sure. Kindling for
the rest of us, but don't let British art's use of Skinhead culture as
convenient way to put racism in a safe place, now past, fool you,
no matter how *Skins* images are dated by background detail (cars,
cans of stout, Woodbine packets), no matter how pristine-perfect
is the production-values of Meadows' film (which I watched with
white folk who alternately laughed at the dumb Asians & cried
for the poor whites whilst I simply seethed behind my fingers).
The suggestion of both mediocre works is that Asian and white
culture will always fundamentally be in opposition, that the lie of
multiculturalism has simply painted over cracks that are still
there. In those moments straight after the latest kid has spat at
you, or the latest drunk twat or sober England-fan has hollered
some racist vitriol in your direction, you could almost believe
that yourself. But once your breathing calms down, and the fear
of the situation has subsided, you remember that multiculturalism isn't a *concept* for some of us, for most of us. Politicians,
particularly Cameron and his cabal of cunts, talk about multiculturalism's 'failure' without realising that in effect he's seeking to
erase our history, the true history of this isle. For most of us
multiculturalism isn't just a sociological idea, it is the only way of
life we've ever known. There is a much stronger history we ALL
have in the UK of simply always being surrounded by, and being

friends and lovers and playmates with, people from all over the planet. Up to a point, I have to admit racism's part in making me, that's how I've learned to be more English than you'll ever be, but here be my pedigree, chum, and it's a bit more complex than any cultural-theorist I've ever read can envisage.

OK, I'm Indian but I'm Cov born'n'bred, weak in the arm and thick in the head. My name, Neil, in Sanskrit, is the colour of Krishna's skin, a shadowing blue as we face down another decade, a darkening blue as my blood thickens and coagulates and seizes up in the dim presentiment of how the likes of me, made up only of the spaces in-between cultures, are a dying breed, stranded by our dislocation. That dislocation increases with age, even if the future generations of people who are going to call themselves proud to be British will be similarly composed of phantom solidity, but in numbers will find STRENGTH from that non-alignment with the monolithic, the strength us nervous pioneers had to keep locked up, sipped from in those moments alone after the freshest latest despair. When we didn't have the advantage of numbers, our music made us strong, gave us voices upon voices, calling us back, pushing us on. On this island so ripe for invasion, so needing of overthrow I've been watching you all my whole life, fascinated by the spectacle of wholeness, white skin, black skin, so pure and sure, so past being a laughingstock, so distant from my fear and resentment. The pop you made, made me, but now it's in glut and decline I look around for a likeness and find nothing. No wonder Asians wanna blow shit up if there's no pop around to suck up their questions and anger and make it art, if in fact their idiot teachers and gurus and imams are teaching them the lie that the prophet hates music, that god disdains the godlike, that poetry can't save your life, that music can be tethered to something as permanent and paltry as a nation or faith. Dislocated on buses on planes on foot in streets and shops and schools and shop floors that barely-disguised loathing and faint-amusement we've been getting since the 30s, through the 60s and 70s that are apparently UK-pop culture's golden age, amplified post 11-9 to a frenzied tinnitus of native anxiety about us - if all that rage created in all those Asian hearts can only find reverb in the words of warmongers and martyrs and priests and not artists then no wonder folk wander onto those same buses and planes and shops with pockets full of dynamite. Music stopped me being a martyr. I had PE to raise questions. And songs to remove my need for answers. Songs that tell you life's a jail. That we're only alive when lost. Songs like *Jag He Bandishala*, from the 1960 Marathi movie *Jagachya Pathivar*, a Chaplinesque tale of a simpleton, a blinded girl and the gangster who kidnaps and blinds her – as is common in much Marathi film by the 60s, the plot is merely the stitching that holds the astonishing score together, one of Sudhir Padke's finest, a soundtrack so good it makes you forget the racist allegiances he has back in your parents' homeland. The song itself is the highlight, the music an almost levitating swell of resigned melody, the lyrics a heartbreaking vision of imprisonment as a metaphor for life, lyrics that for this little misery-guts cut deep back in the day and still do.

"*The world is a jail, all are sinners/everyone has lost their way/Everyone is in love with his jail cell and the cell mates/One even adores his heavy shackles/Everyone restricted to their confines, their vision limited to the fence/Like worms in a fig, they live and die inside/No-one knows the length of their sentence/no one knows where they have come from/his mind panics with the thought of release/he is happier with imprisonment*"

Without songs like that, without the crucial rhizome Marathi song gave and gives me to the reason I'm here, I'd be the means to my end, prone to any suggestions that might ease the anger in my head when all around is condescension and diagnosis and dismissal. Nostalgia is different if your skin's a different colour.

There's the same emotions, embarrassment, joy, regret, but they're amped by that queer relationship with your identity which isn't just about finding out where you belong, but figuring out where your sense of non-belonging can belong, somewhere you'll be able to set up shop in your own skin. The UK rap I listened to & eulogised in the 90s so often sounded like Robert Wyatt, P.I.L, Raincoats, Slits, Kevin Ayers, Richard Thompson, Fairport – because like them it, and me, were searching for a dissident British identity, a Britishness that dug deeper back than the Heath/Wilson models rotated everywhere else, pushed further-forward than the games of canonical reiteration coming out of all that denim and dead skin that was Britpop, created for itself a proudly anti-nationalist British identity closer to your skewed vision of your homeland. Thus I hid, and still oft-hide in a vintage Englishness, in old English books and films and music, not to find comfort but to find a queasy disenchantment with contemporary England that mirrors my own (yes, in a lot of ways I AM the Asian Morrissey). And by the time you're an adult that fearful retrospect, that weary vigilance, that taste of bit-lips, the bile, the hot faced cheek burning shameful paralysis of shock (at the day-to-day scorn & revulsion that still, no matter how imagined, I feel and absorb and add to the inner-shitpile) has been so enmeshed you wonder if you can define yourself without it. By the time my 20s come and go in a blur of pissed & fucked paranoia about kids laughing at my bent shape, race & its infinite regresses into the mind had become a spiral I couldn't escape. Songs can sometimes be the only thing to pull you out of that maelstrom, to remind you that you look up at the same sun and sky and moon as everyone else, to remind you that your mortality is the only thing that will stop the journey, that you're older than your age and ancient by birth.

The real lasting scar that racism can leave is that it can get you to a point where you wonder if your identity is dependent upon the hatred that identity has attracted all its life, you wonder if you're made by racism, and part of you resists the ability of all that hatred to so foretell your future and delineate your fragile sense of self. It makes you a tad mental. It means that everyone tells you your whole life that you're over-reacting, that you're being ridiculous, wonder why you can't just be cool about it, wonder why you're so horrified when you see the Asians who arrived later than your parents engage in precisely the same kind of brainless resentment of new immigrants that my parents had to battle before them. Right now, if you wanna find a racist, go talk to an orthodox Sikh about Muslims, go talk to a 70s-immigrated Hindu about Africans, boggle at how much has been forgotten, how quickly the immigrant hates those who follow their journey, the extra numbers they feel put their security and integration under threat, the way their fitting in is something they feel they've gotten away with, a fitting-in they want to pursue to its logical conclusion whereby they can hate immigrants and new-comers as much as any other Englishman. Spirals of pain within spirals of pain - racism, and the spectres it sends skittering and shattering across the ice inside you, also means that today's Tefal-brow talk of ghosts and hauntings rings awful lukewarm in the twitching traumatised tomb my head's in. What do you do when you don't know how to not be haunted? When you yourself feel like an apparition of a soul containing a hologram of a heart, too broken by now to ever hum whole again. When those ghosts so wispishly and wordily wended around by theorists have stalked next to you your whole life, have made your insides judder and clatter at every step, lurk round every corner, every street you've ever walked down and every house you've ever called home? What do you do when being haunted isn't a construct or a concept or a theory but an everyday reality that keeps you addicted to your alien-ness, secretly dependent on other's revulsion, the crossed street, the change dropped from a distance to your foul palm, the eyes never lying when they tell you just how 'tolerated' you are? Haunted by who you are, by the idea of being someone. I don't lend vinyl any more but there's a song at the heart of this. It's a song sung by a dead woman, a ghost to her husband, warning him that wherever he goes and whoever he's with she will be in his heart. It's soundtracked by vamping keys, insanely heavy reverb, spooked and startling sound fx and was made in about 1965, (just before Marathi song started being bulldozed out of Indian cinema, just before my mum and dad decide to blow Mumbai for the other side of the world) for the film *Paath Laag* and is called *Ya Dolyanchi Don Pakhare*. When I hear this song, in this room, I recall last breaths, the zip of a body bag and I know who's watching me. I know that he faced far worse than I have. And I know that he never had an enemy.

Of course, you could call that a hauntology of my own domestic creation. Clutching at forest tendrils, trying to remember, just another old romantic trying to feel alive again before the Great Uploading. Maybe so. Today fly your flag England . Celebrate. Reveal yourself. As you continually have revealed yourself. As wonderful. And shameful. Both. Accept it. Shame is easy believe me. Take it. It's good for you. It's good for everyone. And the wonder of this isle? I see it all around me. See, there's a place I keep mentioning that isn't England or India or quite like anywhere else. The place I love. The place that truly, eternally, made and mirrors me. Hope in the stones. Hopelessness always two steps on but still, an experiment from the ashes, cauldrons round the lake, cranes now. Funny people. And always new people , too mixed up a place to not have a dead strong identity. Coventry. Coventry my home. Coventry my favourite place on the planet, the only place where I make sense to myself, the only place to always welcome me back with supreme disinterest, to vanish my turmoil in it's own. Always cameras and the clouds are mountains and the grey sky the ocean.

If Cov was just the concrete jungle of its rep perhaps things'd be simpler. It'd just be a smaller Birmingham, and we'd accept our satellite-state to England's 2nd city, wait for the inevitable merger in about 50 years and be happy to simply retain 'business-park' status. But the split between Coventry & Brum, and indeed Coventry and every other town around it isn't just down to football teams or civic-pride, it's deeper in the psyche of Coventry-people because as survivors of the endlessly butchered experiment that is this city, we've emerged with an entirely unique set of attitudes, an entirely local set of broken expectations that somehow seems to be inherited swiftly by everyone who comes here to stay. To me, Coventry is paradise. A post-war experiment in social engineering gone feral, a medieval whisper, a madhouse. I've been an inmate all my life. There are wings I don't wander into, pockets of rights-for-whites belligerence, but that's the same for everywhere now - the bulk of the city is deeply and intrinsically cosmopolitan, constantly changing it's make up, living everyday disproof of Churchill's lies and Cameron's snide asides. Crucially the city hides very little, either about the dreams it had or the dishonest way those dreams have been derailed and defaced by successive waves of hostility from governments whether in the Reichstag or Whitehall. Prod any old fart sinking real ale in one of Cov's more medieval boozers (the Windmill down Spon Street's a good bet) and he'll tell you that 'what Hitler couldn't finish, the council did', but truth be told Coventry has been vandalising itself, ravaging itself naked to welcome new dawns and see new horizons, for 100s and 100s of years. Our eerie avoidance of medieval fire meant thousands of timbered buildings from the 13-hundreds on survived, unlike most ancient towns in England. From roundabout the 1600s we've been tearing it all down on an almost non-stop basis, widening roads, destroying priories and other places of pilgrimage, annoying our neighbours until they come take a pop at the city walls, bulldozing and demolishing to make way for more cars and more car-factories, all waved through past residents' grumblings by careless signatures from Aldermen and councillors and city-engineers. By the mid 30s Donald Gibson & Ernest Ford in the Coventry architects' department had pedestrianised precincts & that fatal split between people and cars planned well before the Luftwaffe lashed the city with fire and genocide. Plans worked out with their wives on their living-room carpets but plans nonetheless, plans that the Luftwaffe bought to a point of urgency and need, plans now being rolled-backwards by every city daft enough to copy us, unaware of the ghostly town centres they'd be bequeathing to the future. In 1936 the ghost-town couldn't be seen for all the hope and the high-mindedness, an editorial in the Midland Daily Telegraph gives us an inkling of the mindset, well before the skies were darkened by Junkels or Heinkels or Messerschmitts: *"Coventry is now emerging from the shackles of a purely utilitarian era, ...an era of commercial revolution allied with civic stagnation...Generations of bad planning - slums, narrow streets, overcrowding, sewers - all the trouble saved up for the future from an unimaginative past must be tackled."*

The new Labour city council set up the Architects dept. in 1938 and the week-long Coventry of Tomorrow exhibition in May 1940 gave Coventry people a chance to see Gibson's plans. Immediately clear in those preliminary sketches of wide-open roads and perfect grassy verges is that Gibson didn't care about buildings as much as he cared about creating a civic space filled with points of view, filled with spots where the vista of a new age could be viewed clearly. Foresight would've maybe predicted how Gibson's vision would be compromised by not only the populace's preferred uses of all that space, but also the wide-open virgin-turf it was opening up to the unscrupulous and unprincipled. By late 1940, after the first, biggest blitz (although Coventry would remain a bombing target throughout WW2) First Commissioner Of Works Lord Reith is telling the boys on the board that Coventry "is a test case, for Government

& for England". The subtext there is clear – never mind the finance, make this city the future of UK cities, make that phoenix fly. Gibson's first report on his proposals comes out in early 41 and is called *Disorder & Destruction: Order And Design*. Together with his plans is an aerial photo of the pre-war city, sloganned 'This Must Not Happen Again'. Coventry ever since has been a living tableau of how socialist/modernist dreams get fucked up by corporate capitalist reality, and how the people who inhabit those dreams and walk those pastel-sketched visions of the future can end up getting turned into troglodytes, given nothing to survive on amidst the underpasses and flyovers and mosaic subways. The day after the bombing, amid scenes of panic, endemic looting and the near-introduction of martial law the need to redevelop 'boldly and comprehensively' emerged as a new mantra for the city council. They haven't changed the record since.

Ever since, us Coventrians have become used to seeing our future on paper, tantalising visions of our city-that-will-be on the front-page of the Cov Evening Telegraph, the city that will rise from the mess that's been made. Always, Coventrians have looked at these draughts and prophesies aware that compromise and conflict will eventually destroy all that pristine perfection, aware of what fucked-up disappointments we are compared to the smiling obedient automatons that people those charcoal-shaded visions of the new metropolis. Gibson's conception of Coventry is in scenes of space, there's a futurist yet time-frozen stillness to his late 30s sketches of Broadgate and Trinity Street and the City Arcade. They're striking, seductive images, new, rational, scientific views of a city, images that make mass-demolition seem both desirable and necessary, juxtaposing the deficiencies of the pre-war Cov (congestion, pollution and disorder) with the promise of an aesthetically and morally ordered modern city-scape. Sanitised for sure but images that seem to impart an order on the city, emphasising certain facets of urban life, but repressing others in the hope that we'd all willingly frog-slouch our way across the new space, knowing our place under-&-wondrous-at the planner's godlike benevolence. No accident that Gibson was influenced by ancient Egyptian architecture, by the cities built by Pharaoh Akhenaten. There's the same godlike benevolence to his designs, the desire to make the populace into sure and whole individuals within a bigger picture.

When those conceptions hit ground level and started being lived in, everything changed, and Gibson himself ended up bemoaning how where he had wanted to zonally separate out the civic, social and cultural lives in the city, Coventry people, who wanted dog-tracks and pubs and cinemas and speedway and more places to party, knew & insisted that those different functions couldn't be separated. People adapted the planners idealist conceptions of civic space for their own ends, precincts never became places for grown-ups to shop, always places for kids and teenagers to hang-out, cause trouble. Those railings built in civic hope of demarcation and direction, I ended up getting tied to and spat at by 4 kids I had thought were my friends. Those wonderful womb-like subways I ended up getting chased down, pinned down, full strength. Acid and mushrooms and all the other teenage naughtinesses rendered Gibson's vision obsolete for many of us, a decaying picture that never matched our own skewed street-level vision. The view from above the drawing-board and the blueprints, the representation that Gibson thought could be lived in, was simply destroyed by citizens trapped in the view from below, alienated from their city even if it had become a more logical place visually and socially. Cov people instinctively knew that what Cov's redesign was attempting was a quashing of spontaneity, an entirely capitalist reordering of public space for commercial ends. And they kicked back even as they had to let things decay, played and fucked about and hid in the sculpted concrete flyovers and underpasses for what else can a rat in a maze do when the maze starts crumbling, when a blueprint decides that none of us are black or brown or white but all beige or colourless. The only band who ever 'got' that precise mix of frantic hope and under-grinding despair just right were the Specials because they knew that Cov is a surreal place, never as simplistically 'hard' or 'tough' as the fuck-awful likes of The Enemy have characterised it as since. 'More Specials' is still such a cutting record for Coventrians because it so perfectly evokes that mix of 60s tastefulness and contemporary degeneration, how it feels to be progressively impoverished as a people whilst living in already-dated future dreams of sophisticated urbanity, how those messy bits of your family's past, particularly how race has played a role, become things to wear with real pride when you're constantly cattle-prodded into a future that seeks to iron out all difference.

And it wasn't just us that wrecked the city. Government fucked it all up too. As a Coventrian, inveterate distrust of successive parties-in-power is ingrained in you, whether it's Labour laying into immigrants or Tories laying into everyone until the poverty-line becomes something a whole city looks up at. Though Gibson's modernist vision was comprised of beautiful curves, lines and proportions as showcased in all the movie-reels & pictures & maps the council generated during the reconstruction, that council's willingness to let developers plonk sudden deluges of sky-high concrete wherever they wanted, darkening those sunlit walkways and creating new corners of fear, also made the lived-experience of Coventry entirely different, a blight on the memories of the old, the only memory young folk had ever had of the place. Coventrians who were meant to be excited about the rebuild rapidly had more mixed feelings of loss and disinterest, a growing grumble about public art and concrete and brieze-blocks not really addressed by council notice-boards explaining the virtues of all this apparent state- vandalism (that attracted it's own public vandalism almost immediately on point of construction). It's in that dissonance between planners conceptions and residents lives that a new kind of Coventry character emerges as I'm growing up, one that oddly-enough more closely-reflects Cov's millennia-long history of dissidence and anti-authoritarian agitation than the falsely plastered smiles and clear-eyes of the idealist 40s & 50s images. Coventrians now are almost constantly disorientated by their city, dazed and desensitized by the brutal way buildings with memory can disappear seemingly overnight. Our city is a building site and has been for 70 odd years. Our factories and workplaces aren't 'converted', they're simply obliterated, a city made of ground-zeroes and pasts erased, and we've got used to the anger, and the retaliatory disinterest you develop as a response.

Growing up amidst this, I slowly realised that Coventry was the perfect home for my own blasted sense of identity, a place where modernity's hope and the endless cruelty of capital's progress made everyone unsure, gave no rocks to cling to. It was no accident that Coventry folk overwhelmingly welcomed my family (a natural ease in the welcome that made those moments in my childhood where race stepped in, all the more painfully vivid and shocking) because Coventry folk were so blearily, confusedly getting on with survival there was no time for many to hate us, no perfect city for us to despoil, no history that could be pointed at that wasn't already under threat from more powerful forces than a few new pakis in the neighbourhood. Coventry's history, of witches and violence, and mystery and magic and resistance isn't preserved, still lingers with burning lividity in the stones that survive and the air that you breathe, but crucially exerts no over-weening pompous pride to Cov's citizens. We are all part of the same demented experiment-gone-wrong. And no matter where I am, only Coventry makes sense of me, only in Coventry do I feel at home, comfortable, to this day. Every day I walk to work past Swanswell Pool. It's filled with ducks and swans and fish and surrounded by drunks and junkies and you and me. When you look up the hill you see a sea of tower blocks, now near-empty and ready for demolition, you see the shop that when you were a kid had a giant picture of Santa Claus on it ("When I go shopping I go to Hillfields!). You hear a million accents, see a million flyers for bhangra-raves and reggae-shebeens and walk past Polish shops and Ukrainian churches and mosques and temples and gurdwaras & you turn back atop Primrose hill street and see what your city has become. A mess of redevelopment and trees planted in metal but still, those 3 ancient spires, still that Pool that was perhaps the first place anyone round here started calling Cov a city (in the dark ages it was called Babba Lucca and the trees were HQ of a coven of dark-artists). And you feel proud, tearful, every time. Cov is living proof that the speed & cleanliness & spaciousness of the 'city of tomorrow' could never withstand the complexities and ambigu-ities of street-life as lived by Cov's ever-changing, ever-arriving populace. It's an amazing place, a city where ancient blood can still be felt seeping through the earth, no matter how many mannered layers of ready-mix idealism have been piled atop it. In Radford, there's a hill made of blitz-rubble and innumerable unidentified corpses. 300 years from now, you sense Coventrians will stand atop it, watching and waiting for the flood-waters to subside, wondering again, how safety can be created from the latest devastation, knowing all too well how the pedestrian can poetically defy any attempt from above to erase the chaos, knowing how an improvers sky-high-pie zeal can never be stronger than a citizen's ground-level fears.

That's the mindset of the place, and these things I've learned in that ever-ready-for-the-worse mentalopolis that is Cov. Your life is an over-reaction to its roots. Your life has always been bent out of shape by the fact that whatever room you walked in, whatever street you walked down, people noticed your difference. And that difference affects every single relationship you ever have, whether it's with people, places, or the art that ensues. The only difference between you and the natives is that you've been forced to acknowledge the gaps and gulfs and guilt inherent in art, the way that as expressions of personality they're always expressions of identity whether sexual, cultural or racial. A similarly faux-welcoming sense of architectural order was imposed on my early listening by the vinyl bought for us by white friends who called my dad Matty & my mum Rita: Johnny Cash, Geoff Love, Tchaikovsky – despite these well-meaning attempts to make us fit, it was my dad's old vinyl and tapes that dominated our shared listening, that we ran to whilst all around was talk of 'integration'. In a way, those records were an attempt, a generous attempt, like my parents acquiescence in their name-changes, like Gibson's draughts & diagrams, to make us Coventrians forget where we came to the city *from*, and join the blinkered forward vision so busily built around us, the vision Cov's citizens, Irish, Polish, Pakistani, Indian, African have always resisted and destroyed simply through the lives we've led. People are made of more complex stuff than other people's plans for them will ever countenance. Your blackness, your brownness, are monoliths within you and your life is spent in resistance, reflection, rapture in those genes, you're a walking wounded cenotaph to notions of integrity and certitude. But in comparison to your own frantic attempts to find out who the fuck you are, the confidence of your white peers in their birthrights and THEIR nation, can feel surer, steadier but never enviable. Because Christ, if you felt at home your whole life, who the fuck would you have ended up as? That grit in yr cells, that reaction against, IS you. And Coventry, as a place of resistance, as dazed dead-end, as an experiment, as good a place as any, suits you from the top of your head to the soles of your feet. My mum's feet are jungle-hardened, slipped in the unfamiliar snow and broke her arm carrying me, took her to Boots and asked for shoes. Coventry took us in, slow-cooked me in both honest ill-will and serpentine 'understanding' (more hateful, and often from posh cunts from Leamington & other satellite villages) and I sit now, in the room my father died in, hearing the trains scream their midnight prayers to the rails, the sirens zero in on their target, and the songs I'm playing make it plain that in this world, I won't find a home, only a refuge. Fine by me. Cov gives me what little pride I have. Proud to have stayed in the wonderful city that gave my wondering parents a home, proud to be from a city whose only constant is it's constant racial change, the constant ruination of its projected future.

Such ruination we should all be getting familiar with now that capital can't make us believe in old dreams any more, now that the fiction of progress is something we *all* see through. Now that there's nothing left but a massive and endless boiling over of anger. The chunks of the West that were my fascination and I worked for are in terminal decline. The project that was the music-industry that your empires took worldwide, that bought me in Cov's crumbling confines these black plastic lifelines and reels back to my story, is similarly in free-fall and dereliction. In such times, we cling to what we can, me to my city and my tapes but such exit-strategies and homesickness, this need to feel connected again, aren't just my problem any more. We've all been told the future is where we are, and that our pasts are to be got over, energy and entropy aren't just battling in withered old shells like me, every generation of pop fans has it's own no-mans lands to stumble over now, it's own ways out of the sense-killing tyranny of good and bad taste back to the freedom of listening, hearing, believing, feeling, tasting again. We need to see how we're going to escape you from the narrowing cul-de-sac that's squeezing out the dying breaths of Western pop. And to do that you're going to have to take your medicine, taste the poison from your own proud history. Summer's coming and the factory's dying. Hear the whoop-whoop from Little Park St. police-station, the fires, the smashing and grabbing? Hear the city grinding its eyes open? Hear the birds in the black trees? Pretty soon the world out there will be awake to inspect the wreckage. We need to make plans before dawn. I'm staying right here. You've got to move. The next time I speak to you, we may say our farewells.

Chapter 6

Too Dumb Too Amnesiac

Hey. Wake up. You fell asleep. I've been for a walk, down the hill, up the hill, through the entry, past the old school and home again. S'the same walk I took an hour after my dad died, trying to clear my head, finding a daze I've tried to stay in since, worried of what horrors lie in self-realisation. Tonight, on balance, has not been good for me. Dawn will be here soon. My friend came whilst you were out, popped in, he's gone now. He recommended a note by way of explanation. Read it back to me.

Yeah, that'll be fine. Keep that. Do what you want with it, y'know, afterwards. This morning, in a little while, my second life begins. I'm tired of being a critic and I wannabe reincarnated as a human being. Here it is. Hold it. Heavy aint it. Time tough, time tight, *only the rich can get away with theft, and only the police can get away with murder*, a thousand apologies. Did you go to a fucking pub last week, when they were clearing up glass in the street? Did you hear how British people explained things away? Their old remedies of send-in-the-troops barbarity and send-em-back repatriation? Bud bud bud bud. Green cats, cat curries, 7 to a room, stink of curry, kill their women when they're not beating them, hate white people, mean to kill you. A thousand apologies you fucking white cunt, a thousand apologies. How close all these vintage lies are to the surface, how easily they can slip back in cos they have hardly any distance to travel from the bubbling undercurrent of the British mindset to the foreground of public discourse. Only takes a riot for all those old analyses of our propensities to re-emerge in the shitstorm of attempted expla-nation – before we know it we're branded as 'sick', kept in the back of the public mind as the reason Britain is now 'broken', or even worse, Asians become proof of how immigrants can 'make it', emblematic examples of how the hard-working piccannini can become greedy wage-slaves just like everyone else, fit with the programme. The question always asked – why can't black people be like them there nice Asians? A thousand apologies. I've seen the advert, the one where the whole script is divided line-by-line between a representative cross-section of British society, only joined together to say the brand-name at the end, ukuleles emphasising our mutual respect for each others walls and castles. I saw the Asian family in the middle who had the line 'because they can't be beat for price'. I felt the slight cringe. I guess we belong now. I guess I should have nothing to beef about. I guess I have to change my mind again. If I'm allowed.

See, people don't want to merely be 'tolerated' anymore than they want the compromise & cowardice implicit in the word 'integration'. Both of those words suggest that *we're* the problem when we confront racism, that only when the racial aspect of our being is successfully neutralised can we and you move on, it's a way of thinking that supports the long-term habit in the UK of blaming hate on the hated. Selfishly, but like everyone, we want our race to be something we can celebrate, we can explore but that everyone else can shut the fuck up about. When you hear someone protest that they 'can't talk about race' anymore, you can bet that what they want to say about race is critical, hateful, prescriptive for a community who's complexity they're denying even in their supposed straight-talking concern. Deeper than the things you *expect* to be denied as part of a minority (a decent wage, fair treatment, and visibility on screens and billboards and on football pitches) are the things you don't expect – at root the denial of mental or moral complexity, the assumption that your mind can't be changed. When the country doesn't want you, tells you *you've* got a problem about that distaste, it means that everyday you reject and disown whatever you said yesterday, flip the acceptance or refusal of the last 24 hours in a fit of pique. A childish ability to suddenly jettison principles to make the dominant culture guilty at the twists and turns it spins me on, of course the dominant culture barely notices, but it means my mind's a mess caught in a stubborn Möbius between megalith-like sureness and supreme self-loathing. Hey, I ain't as smart as you white folk. You vote out of something other than fear, vote with hope you dumb fucks. Which is how we end up with a slippery cunt like Cameron in no.10, a racist clown like Johnson as Mayor. Hope you dipshits are proud.

Yes I'm angry. Yes I'm retaliating. Just admit. You started it. Heh.

I'm constantly told how much better I should feel about racism in the UK, how much has been improved, how little my kind stand out any more, how much we fit in, how ridiculous it is to 'have a problem' about race any more. Look around, see our undoubted growth in numbers, open my mouth, realise I'm getting too old to stomach my own bile, swallow it back, add it to the inner sludge. I'll admit that Asians are more 'visible' in England's presentations of itself – but we're fkn idiots if we don't realise that internally & domestically we'll still be first port-of-call when a prevailing white mindset needs something to take the piss out of, even if the Great Shittish Public have different nemeses for their anger now. I don't see that now I get 'I'd rather be a paki than a turk' chanted at me on most Saturday afternoons as progress, I don't see that people dumping their race-hate on the more generalised loci of 'immigrants' or 'asylum seekers' as proof that the UK has a 'natural tolerance'. One of the most appalling things to realise in recent years is that Asians have forgotten the struggles our mums and dads had, are able to feel even more British than ever before by joining in the national sport of xenophobia. Some of the most virulent race-hate I've heard in the past few years has come from

Asians themselves, whether directed at other faiths within their own neighbourhood, or at new incomers to those neighbourhoods from Africa or Eastern Europe. The almost comical amnesia of these chuckle-heads in laying into those who've merely followed the same trails they did beggars belief. It's in those African kids, and Polish kids, and Slavic kids that I detect the spark of how I felt back in the day, the commitment to self-education based on mistrust of an education system that can't keep up with them, and a native UK culture that places nothing but distrust and envy on those ambitions of non-inferiority. Without a doubt, Britain is doing a good job of presenting itself as a more tolerant place, is maintaining a slick sheen wherein anyone who even brings race up as an issue is being somehow horrifically dated, trading in vintage race-relations language 'unsuited' for modern discourse, always the spectral threat of 'thought-police' and correctness-gone-mad making sure that racists can feel just as confident in spewing prejudice about asylum seekers or immigrants (two terms handily without colour-suggestions, a bit like 'non-EU immigrants'). The far right that gave me such terrors as a child has won elections, marches the streets with ever-growing strength but yeah, why worry? You pay taxes, you're useful, safe, a grown-up, no longer running from the lynch-mob but watching it from the safety of your sofa. The desperation in the UK to 'finally start talking freely' about race, the perception that for a long time being 'honest' about immigration has been impossible, has led to the new millennium being a time unrivalled in my lifetime for the blatancy and consistency of racist talk in the press and across the media. I teach kids, and I know what an effect this has had, how much is being forgot, what old bigotries are being made gospel again. The less subtle likes of the EDL & BNP perform a useful function for Britain, as the marginal crackpots the mainstream parties can project all racism onto, whilst the mainstream can carry on engaging in precisely the kind of immigration=problem conflation that has animated every single legislative immigration act since the 60s. Everywhere is repeated the great lie: that the people who voted BNP aren't actually racist, only underserved by govt., a mantra popping off from most of the major parties ever since before the 2010 non-election. This notion that the Great British Public instinctively don't have it in them to be racist when the truth is that there is endemic racism within the UK whipped up by a hysterical press and a political mainstream unwilling to confront it. Coconuts like Baroness Warsi, perpetuate that condescending attitude that oh - if you're white and poor voting for a fascist party is an excusable response (no it fucking isn't), actually seeming to believe her own horseshit about how her constituents are 'concerned' about how the govt. is 'under-resourcing' immigration. Whenever anyone (and everyone does) talks about "caps", "tighter controls" and about how it's what the Great British Public wants it's the same ol'shit that's been spewed out since the Smethwick result in the 64 election i.e. parties realising that race-hate and prejudice is a vote-winner and tacitly diluting/soft-soaping those racist policies accordingly. The only difference in 2011 is that it's apparently those nasty Eastern Europeans we should be sendin' back. This country NEEDS invasion, the flood, the swamp, the deluge just to shake us into this fucking century, to make us grow the fuck up, to break the cowardice and cravenness of the political mainstream & the way that the tyranny of 'public opinion' actually muddies and obfuscates any real-talk about race/immigration in this country because we've all got to tiptoe around the racism in England's heart, the racism England will deny forever. Since the twin towers fell, and alongside the new crusades our brave-boys have been fighting since, that inherent prejudice has got a whole lot fucking worse for the likes of me in offices, school playgrounds, the street, and the papers. This old son-of-immigrants finds himself perhaps more secure than ever in my hidey-hole, but increasingly aware that by 'joining' mainstream UK culture you're invited to salute some utter bullshit: the search for a 'solution' to immigration, the entire 'debate' resting on the assumption that it is a 'problem'. Peripheral parties blame the mainstream ones for not 'facing up to it', mainstream parties bleat amongst themselves about who is best 'dealing' with that problem. At all times the language and phraseology is medical, mirrors Bal Thackeray's desire to cut out and excise immigration to make the nation well again. It's best to remember what you should've always remembered – that you've lived in Britain all your life and perceive NO fucking 'problem' with immigration other than the entirely unjustified rancour and resistance from the 'natives'. When you start investigating that rancour you'll see NO concrete or valid arguments, merely red-top snarl and gibber, 'quality dailies' fear and loathing, broadsheet bleating about 'sustainability', the take-our-jobs/jump-the-queue/dilute-our-culture bullshit I've heard all my life. As ever, that general distaste/repulsion with the different languages/cultures people find themselves encountering is never directly confronted or questioned, just worked around, appealed to, the 'these terrorists want to ban Xmas'-level of discussion never risen above. It worries me as a parent, and as a teacher, but I'm also aware that the young have a vigilance, and a way of knowing when they're being lied to, that frequently shames the older generation, including the supposedly sensitive likes of me.

A student of mine directed me towards his favourite youtube video of the moment yesterday, in fact wanted me to show it to the whole class. I quickly discovered that this massive youtube hit was called 'Muslim Demographics' and was a ton of ill-sourced bullshit posted by someone called friendofislam (who it turns out is an evangelical US Christian). I showed the class on the big screen, like my dad leaving the downstairs doors open so I could hear the argybargy uncensored, asked them what they thought. Yes plenty of 'I like immigrants except the one's who won't learn our language . . . . ' - we're now dealing with a younger generation with daft young parents & inevitably short memories about the racist history of the UK, who have fundamentally had their notions about immigration dictated/effected by nigh-on a decade of press hysteria/horseshit and a generalised notion that Islam is out to wreck us all. However there were also kids watching the video who challenged it, either from knowledge or a righteous sense of when they could spot they were being fucked with or played by someone. They did so however, almost fearfully, worried about what the majority of the class would think of them. When I, unable to zip-it, waded in and started accusing kids of being EDL fodder I got shouted down, quite rightly. That ingrained consensus about England being under threat, those deeper, no more-palatable but way more presentable prejudices about the 'disappearance' of Englishness are the real battle in this country, not the loonytoons fucknuttery of the EDL. There's plenty of understanding amongst kids, especially the latest wave of Polish and Eastern European kids, that immigration 'control' might be a problematic concept because it always gets tied in with the racial fears of it's epoch – these people are now looking homeward because we've become such tiny-minded nimby fucks that anyone (oh - apart from the 'most skilled' of course) who seeks a home here has to be instantly treated with suspicion, has to doff their hat as much as they can to British 'tradition' and 'civilization' or else they're ripe for deportation/detention, watched for what benefits they dare to take from us native taxpayers. Blacks in the 50s, Asians in the 60s, Ugandan Asians in the 70s, Kosovans & Bosnians in the 80s/90s, eastern Europeans now - I don't see how current talk about immigration 'control' isn't just as motivated by fear and hysteria as previous shitstorms. Crucially in my day to day life I don't actually notice immigrants 'damaging' the supposed rose-garden that is British society at all, and I can't be the only one who feels that mismatch between media-hysteria and the ease of those relationships as lived. Any teacher you speak to who's had to teach Polish kids or African kids in the last few years will probably tell you that they work a fuck of a lot harder than our supposedly squeezed-out British kids and I'd suggest that it's only when Britain stops feeling fucking sorry for itself, realises it's not 'entitled' to any kind of fealty or reverence just because it has a history, that its people will start bucking those trends and smartening up as much as immigrants to the UK have to to survive.. This repel-all-borders notion that there are 'no controls' at the moment, and that we are in a constant crisis has passed from the front pages of the Tory-rags to something approaching a national consensus and I just don't see its accuracy at street-level. I see racist graffiti smeared where Polish kids gather, graffiti written by Asian kids too dumb, too amnesiac, too dumbly parented to know what old-games & roles they're stepping into. I have to button my lip when talking to English-born Asians like me whose command of English is so much poorer than their African & Eastern European peers. We've become as blatheredly uncaring about Englishness as the English.

In such a situation, in such a country so addicted to its own bullshit, sometimes I start thinking that only one thing will save us. Fucking. And babies. Serious.

It's the way life is led, that will destroy as much of racism as it's possible to destroy. We're heading for a time in the UK where non-whites will be more diffuse and present than ever. Cunts like Starkey & Theresa May may fear that time, but there's no legislating against love - once we've all spent a few decades getting along and getting it on there'll be a ruling class of pure-white pink-necked scum running things and the rest of us under-neath, who are gonna be every colour under the sun, waiting for our kids to want or seek that power, making sure those kids know that the meek ain't gonna inherit shit and if they want power they're gonna have to take it. We're heading that way now, I teach younger kids, 16/17 year-olds born in the mid-90s who genuinely seem to be approaching a state in which they don't even notice colour, whose whole lived life has been one of diversity, where race only gets mentioned when the older members of the family insists on reminding them, racial characteristics merely a series of jokes and knowing pisstakes, race only being something they're made aware of when pulled into rituals by their parents that mark them out as belonging to a past or a homeland, whether that's an Somalian wedding or a Pakistani funeral or an Irish wake or a Jamaican party . I'm sure I should be seeing those kids as some kind of lost cause, perhaps precisely those who need reminding of race and what it means. But, really, those kids remind me of how far, & how short, navel-gazing can get you. Everyday I realise that turning yourself inward too much, endlessly asking "who you are" (am I black am I white am I gay am I straight am I a feminist... the excuses for inertia this endless self-pity gives you) might just be a crutch, that perhaps it's more important to realise who you are is best proven by what you do, your part in the struggle and everything else. To that extent, I have no 'problem' with white folk any more, I married one, and we made lovely white & brown babies. I only have a real fkn problem with you whether you're 16 or 96 if you mindlessly serve up the shit you've been taught, if you think people who come here should 'respect' the flag, learn the language, kowtow and doff their cap to you just cos you were 'lucky' enough to be born here. The language is still what I most love about England. A living model of all we've shared, and how Englishness, once, meant precisely an openness to the world, a world that encountered not just hatred from British people, but curiosity and a willingness to learn that undercut the more institutionalised chauvinism.

We've shared a lot my friend, for all the different tangents things sent us on, for all the self-inflicted & imposed difference of vantage points, we should both hopefully be able to see this glorious dunderheaded genius country we love for what it is. My England was not your England, although we shared its streets, a laugh, a smoke, a drink; you've been my best friend. But right now, stretched out under the same orange skies as you, watching night get its brightness and contrast pumped back into dawn's undimming by a remote god's remote control, we both must see that this is our England now - to be fought for, to be defended against itself. It's an England holding a torch for a Britannic imperial past built on exploitation, slavery, colonialism, indenture and immigration. It's an England perhaps only just waking up to how ideas rather than economics are what makes racism real these days, how racist idea and racist act are so difficult to delineate in this intermediary state we're in between flesh'n'bone and fibre-optic. What we're seeing in 2011 repeatedly from press and politicians is an attempt to slap on, impose from above a sense of British values on the nation, almost entirely cosmetic, and yet fanning embers that glow with shame and fear and division and street-level nastiness. In 2011 my Marathi-song reveries are imbued with a yearning, a desire for escape I might've thought would've lifted by the time I was 40. Didn't work out that way. Need to hide now more than ever. Easier to dance alone than pretend you belong. Both are bad habits.

The popular hatred of asylum seekers is guided by the new Islamophobia that is the theoretical & rhetorical arm of racism in 2011, the rationale that justifies what's currently seething on our streets, and we can't allow the battle against those ideas to undermine or over-intellectualise that concrete daily struggle. Any immigrant - 2nd-gen or otherwise - has to realise that, increasingly, the brutishness that is Britishness isn't held together by anything coherent, but more stitched up by fear of an enemy within, whether that fear is found in the sophistry of the liberal middle-classes or the red-top tactics of the tabloids and the EDL. Britain, like so much of old Europe, lusts for the brands and ravishments of globalisation but can't stomach seeing the new-folk it brings (and really can't stand it when those bar-coded happiness-objects get stole by those mongrel hordes, without having the dignity to be 'declared' like MPs expenses were). Politically, racism is still useful to every party as a way of explaining hardship, promising redemption through toughness. Of course, Asians - Marathi, Punjabi, Sikh, or Gujarati - are as guilty as anyone else in accepting the current racialization of religion, perpetuating it in the temple and the gurdwara and the street. We're not talking about easily search-lit fascists any more: the classless suffusion of Islamophobia from the graffiti on the walls to talk-radio chat to youtube comments sections to Hindu Sikh pamphleteering to the prime-ministers speeches shows how the politics of fear is currently winning the hearts and minds of all classes in this country, whether it's bourgeois fear of the immolation of a spurious national culture of 'tolerance', or alleged working-class fear of aliens thieving jobs, homes, shops and their kids futures.

At work, seeing Coventry's ever-dizzying new waves of new people come and go, I see reasons to smile, reasons to scowl. Without a doubt the kind of isolation that turned me out rarely exists any more. But in my lifetime, in terms of how acceptable on a street-level racist language and action is, shit's not got better, not progressed. There is no moving on. Shit's got WORSE as institutions find better ways to hide their inveterate prejudice, as individuals turn the mere suggestion that they might have to moderate their language and behaviour into an angry retaliatory rejection of political care that liberates the inner bigot, more free than s/he's ever been to walk this sceptred isle smearing their racist shit on the ever-growing walls between us. It's down to us to dismantle and destroy the bullshit being built in the name of Britishness, whether it's in black and white on a newspaper page or policy draft, or between black and white people on the street, on the march, or on the rampage. The more I listen to the music of my parents youth, the less I feel like getting trapped in my past, the more I feel like taking a leaf from their courage and clarity of purpose. In 2011 the politics of identity cannot trap us inside ourselves when there are battles out the front door, when the apparatus of the state is becoming so informed by whom the fuck THEY think WE are. The word shouted at me 10 years ago was bomber, and until a few months ago Osama was quite a common one too. To the English idiot, any Asian could be a Muslim, every Muslim is a fundamentalist, and anyone wearing a headscarf or a beard a malefactor within the gates.

It's not art's *duty* to combat that idiocy. But great Asian art does so all the time. Crucially, Indian music at its best reminds me that I had music before I had words or categories for it: at its best, it suggests to me that it's time I shut the fuck up about music and spend a few years just listening, care less about having the final word than quietly exploring those moments for which there aren't words, let those folk who mistake music for the accumulation of taste have their lists and lineages and things You Must Hear Before You Die whilst I get busy finding out what and HOW I must hear before I can start living again. I have no idea what this new music will sound like, or how it will unfold, but I'm absolutely convinced that a look east in a spirit of innocence and discovery is essential, an admission that our present is a prison, that a while spent absorbing and adapting could give us an open future preferable to an eternity of knowing and nailing down the Western models we've so thoroughly exhausted. We have to relax our notions of music, just as we must relax our notions of nationality. Before we surrender to brand-Britannia, everyone in the fortress should be wary of how our new god the market tries to erase history, peddles false pasts, confines what can be said: in the past 10 years white English pop should feel fucking ashamed of its silence, the way it's allowed the creeping fear and loathing in contemporary public discourse on race to simply sail into the mainstream with nary a whisper against, no counter-statement bar an endlessly bleated insistence that hey, race doesn't matter, that the 'universality' of songs about relationship and romance is enough of a response. Your general subject, love, is MINIMAL motherfuckers, and isn't arming anyone - the maximum ambition of British pop at the moment is to be a DISTRACTION from what the fuck is really going on. Radios 1,2 & 6, The NME & everyone else in the music-press, should be scraping their skin off in abject fucking guilt and shame about this. You silent, dumb, wretched treacherous fucks. I learned to write about music in a 30 floor building filled with magazine-offices, one of about 4 to 5 people who were black/Asian who weren't pushing a tea-trolley about. I don't think those ratios have changed much since. The same old story, the same old white-domination and exploitation, Jessie J sweeping the boards at the MOBOs, don't fucking tell me ANYfknthing's been sorted. The pop industry is racist because from top to bottom it pussyfoots around the racist 'taste' of it's mainstream audience - and to a huge extent that's the entire history of pop in a nutshell. The pop industry is racist because pop is founded in a racist country, the US - rock & roll was the process whereby the stink of slavery got forgot by some, driven home harder to others, sometimes seemingly/magically absconded but never really left, unspoken now but still the template of the entertainment power-structure we all suckle from. Rock & roll's initial pleasure lay precisely in its essentially failed cultural tourism, white rednecks hampered in their attempts to play black music, vacillating between self-realisation and denial. And in that failure, that furnace of history... such joy and greatness, sure, but don't forget the hierarchy, don't forget the segregation, the assumed superiority, the backdrop, the racial COLLISION at the heart of rock & roll's birth pangs, and the unmannered, brutal way that collision unpicked itself, the enduring way western pop is still pretending that hostilities are at a cessation, that it doesn't still have some seriously twisted issues with people from ex-empire, or new accession countries, even if it's lovin' and theiving and reissuing what they produce. You only have to look at the way reggae musicians have been fucked over and forgotten by precisely the reissue market that lionises their work to realise that just because fanboys are involved, just because the rape of this music is being conducted by people with blogs who call themselves 'fans first and foremost' doesn't mean the same old games of imperialist pillage aren't being enacted, even if it's not big corporations doing it but some spod sticking mediafire links into a wordpress engine. Today's fucknutted new-age music futurologists, confident that when music becomes a mere utility that flows like water all these old injustices will somehow be erased, are sticking their heads in their own manure, doolaley on their own fermented suppurations: don't expect the new interactive-Media empires and multinational entertainment corporations to end the same old tale of black innovation and white exploitation. Why should they? It's what profited the traditional music industry they're strip-mining into obsolescence, the old structures they're gonna step into garbed in hipper, more 'fan-friendly' clothes. The gap-year pastiche playfulness with the bloody roots of pop now being enacted by the middle-class currently dominating UK music (artists, industry & press) serves to render all history equally neutered, recast in a world where 'only the song' or 'only the passion' matters. Fuck that. In the beginning of pop was that n-word I can't say (a word I still find offensive, especially when jokingly quoted by non-African Americans) and we're all here as a result. 60 years on since the Empire, since the birth of pop, the current instant-availability of all music forces some questions on all of us. And sometimes the answers can come from the most unlikely sources, for me from a bundle of tapes in an attic, and a memory of magic I still can't explain.

We're slowly coming to terms with the fact that music's

history is longer than that of the recording industry, that we're all back in a world where musicians travel, throw their cap down, hope for the best. The Marathi music I've been listening to and loving my whole life came to my ears via the magic of recording - was only accessible to this distant whelp through the technology bought to my parents' homeland (India) by the putsch of MY homeland (Britain). But what this music proves is that there's something older than empires - something inherent and intrinsic to the way music is made and used in the East - that might just be the only way forward for western musicians, the only way out of these smart-arsed, burnt-out ruins we're in. Before the industry can con us that merely with a little more of our re-financing they can give us gold again, let's step back, lets realise with the old music of the West we have to remember what internal patterns of conquest and exploitation were going on within our borders - we're fucking chumps if we just sup up the endless classic-version of pop's past without tasting the brackish backdrop, smelling the charnel-house smoke, realising who was gaining and who losing in this evil deal. The history of Western pop is the history of racism on an industrial and cultural scale. Now the entire history of recorded-sound is a click away, we need to be more careful than ever to notice who and what is getting played when the needle drops or the laser lingers or the file gets play listed, what deeper part of history is getting forgot in our agility over its wreckage. And if that relationship at pop's heart, the conversation and confrontation between black Africa and white America is feeling played out, does pop music even exist any more on that ground or is it confined and imprisoned, paralysed by it's refusal to see the blinkered mess it's in, the back-story we can never read again because the future-now is all that is foregrounded, the possibilities we can't explore because the dead-end of pop-historical lies clamp us into old modes of habitual rapacity. Pop is a racial wound unhealed, and I'm in no mood to make light, forget, and pretend it ain't so. Pop, for all its pleasures, done fucked me up and I've squeezed it dry and I want out. I have no sunny reminiscence, no self-pity stronger than my self-loathing, no amusing Anglo-Indian mutual-misunderstandings that could stretch to a half-hour of comedy, no community I grew from except for a secret society keeping something Vedic alive, something in Sanskrit, dying tongues and mantras only my kind could say or understand, no-one to thank bar my parents, in love, who made me a home, once they'd changed their names for ease of pronunciation, once they're realised how resistance isn't a single act but a lifelong act of being.

Caught by the old ghosts, dimly guinea-pigging the future I, like you, am one of the fans that won. We won. We won what exactly? The right to find our listening coasting on round the same atrophied corners again and again, the east only looked at once it starts thieving from us, once it has the post-colonial confidence to remind us of things we know. The right to explore a strictly filtered pop universe that blinds us to the musical multiverses that we might swim in were we to drop the shoulder, admit ignorance, stop look and listen rather than keep closing our eyes for the old rushes of our pasts, hear instead pasts we can't access directly via our own, other ways of being music makers and listeners. In the writers block of 2010 it was an admission of defeat that gave liberation, a defeat with a hope that through naïve and innocent exploration of things like the classical and cinematic back-roads I've outlined above, that we might be able to hear rather than process again. And thus find a way to genuinely free music from fear, to let it touch again the natural ease and innocent movement of our day-to-day relationships with each other. Our chance to enact the vanishing of the racist music industry from the music we choose to listen to offers that opportunity, as does our vigilance at rejecting those interpretations of music that seek to force it to sing for those racists and bigots always on the look out for music they think can reaffirm their messages of hate and division. The destruction of the music industry, the death of criticism offers us the chance to dig the past present and future in an honest, open way, discover that the only way out of dead-end-now is not to lower our expectations of music but to change them, realise that finding a music that we can live with might be more important that finding something that makes our jaws drop or our pants drop or our friends admire us more. Ditch the hyperbolic response we're conditioned to expect/expectorate in favour of a more subtle invasion and revolution of our everyday. Realise that a commitment to music's future means we're gonna have to really apprehend all aspects of music's history, realise that the history of the record-industry is one that spans roughly about 2 human lifespans and that's *all*, stop thinking we have so little time and too much to hear. Start thinking about how we hear, and how we use that time.

I haven't really ever calmed down to the point of being able to do that, to the point, perhaps of feeling the same tranquillity and wholeness that my parents felt when hearing these songs. They felt connected, returned, when they heard these songs, when I heard them they merely added to the powerful disconnect I felt, the sense that what I had to live up to was too enormous for me to comprehend. Without my parents ease and grace with their birthrights, their non-doctrinal passing on to me of what they could, I might've rejected it, or worse, taken it on in an entirely dogmatic way that would end in my refusal and resistance of it. Parenthood makes you think about your parents, and I have grown to realise that there's a lot I should be thankful for. Who I am, who I was born as, has brought me strife, from my skin inwards but my own self-sanctimony is part of it as well, and that can't be blamed on anyone but myself and the music and books and movies I've indulgently been drowning myself in for so long, all that art that so encourages that self-rhapsodizing delight in your own melancholy. As you grow older you realise that the open-ears you have to have as a critic, have also let in a lot that's angered you, that's maybe got you addicted to your own anger in a way not helpful, in a way that might have stopped you growing up. You also, as you grow, realise that there's plenty of people you've put on the 'other side', who have way way more problems than you, problems perhaps even more intractable than the colour of their skin. People without families. People whose families are so fucked up they offer no refuge. Just cos you feel your problems were unfairly inflicted upon you, doesn't mean rage and pain and agony can't hurt just as much or more when not inflicted by a race but inflicted by a careless mother, or an errant father, or a bastard of a brother. We've all got shit to get over, true liberation I think comes from realising you'll never get over anything, never 'deal' with bereavement and anger and loss, and never deal with the racism of the UK you feel has blighted you into the weird corner you're in now, any more than you can wipe out the UK's history. History isn't an excuse for feeling sorry for yourself or any reason to stop struggling; it always provides vivid contradiction to that exhausted, sulky inertia. Just because the million-year old mystery that is music is finally snapping itself out of a 150 year old daydream wherein it was bar-coded and blown-up, and everyone in any way tangentially connected to that biz is bricking themselves, doesn't mean it can't survive, return to another state again, or a new state of an old disorder. I think two things will make this happen. People talking. And music made with way more humility and deeper ambitions than simply visibility or self-idealisation. Creativity not just in what we can make but how we listen to others. Realising that us 'minorities' have our own history of prejudices to battle. Realising that to be an adult is ultimately to shed those lies that shored up your adulthood, free swim again in some doubt, wonder, and openness again. Soon you'll see. I'm finally growing up. Trying to anyway. Trying to find a new way to be an adolescent. A new way to maybe stop looking down at my feet and start facing up to the path ahead.

I suggest it to myself as a critic, because being a pop critic is never about pure reportage, it's about also knowing ways you think music *should* work, *should* look, *should* sound and presenting those ideas stylishly. But this music, and other music from places pop isn't looking (see appendix) doesn't give you that freedom, that chance for you to put your ego between you and it. It demands that you listen and find a new way of responding, perhaps a way that isn't even verbal or physical but more intimate than that, more linked in with the way you live your life, the way you find a live worth living. It's music that points to no future I can delineate before it occurs, and that's perhaps the most exciting thing about it, that it insists music is not made by auteurs or stars or artists but by people, places, and systems. That to me has way more inherent possibilities for our future as musicians and listeners than simply trying to be the next important band, the next important star, the next chapter in a story who's premise is racist, who's body is essentially tragic, who's conclusion is an endless forgetting. With your tastes growing sour from the rich plenitude on permanent offer from your screen and your home, this might be a good thing, with the perma-collapse of the industry and the underground's endless attempts to replicate the same structures in miniature this might be a good thing, music you can't possess that possesses you, music that goes further than mere possession. A playlist stranded in time that can never grow, a playlist that could be endless but that more often shrinks down to a single song that matters today, this morning, tonight, songs you have to replay (anathema though that is to these crammed busy-learning-nothing times) because they reach further in to exert a quieter, more meditative hold on you. I suggest it to myself as a way to make listening a surprising act again. Pass me the gun. It doesn't kill people, only critics, and when I pull the trigger I'll be free to be a person. To hear without having to make my own noise. I'd say 'person again' but I've never been a person.

I can't wait to see what it's like."

I suggest it to you because I love you. Because you're my friend, and that's why you came here. Soon the critic dies, but before then a handshake, a farewell. Because we're living proof that growing up never was about finding out who you are. Just about making sure who you aren't, who you're not gonna stand alongside, who you're going to share your impure bastard-past and fucked-up future with. Sorry to have kept you so long. Let our eyes meet on the nearest star through the silhouetted branches. At the start of a new day of Eastern Spring. The summer soon come. How curious that this ring of steel on my temple somehow feels less real than it did in my daydreams. Despite our differences, because of our differences, for us both it's about survival now. And whim.

Vultus oriens, Ecce Homo Sacer, Rodus Dactlyus Aurora I don't have long so listen now, before your house wakes and time starts stealing your future again an ancient song for a new dawn. Hear the sun?

Look away. No one to blame. A whim.

Hear the noise it makes?

Feel it in your heart.

Postscript: Radio Golha, 2008, Plan B Magazine.

I wrote this piece in 2008 and indirectly it led to the beginnings of the writing contained in 'Eastern Spring'. Iranian music, especially given my mother's mythical ancestry, is perhaps my next area of exploration, and I'm finding it, as with Indian music, still inexhaustible, still inspirational, still incredible. The Radio Golha site is still functional but I would recommend joining the Golha facebook group to hear even more.

Lately, I've been transfixed by a transmission I have no desire to stop listening to. Crucially, listening, I have no desire, because every desire my heart ever had is expressed far clearer than I ever felt it in what I'm hearing. There's something about the music on Radio Golha that makes it perhaps the most violent assault on your ongoing desensitisation to sound, a reconfiguring of your most ingrained listening habits, and a factory-default reset of your expectations when you retune to Radio Realworld, like a fallen angel, a wiped-away tear. In an age where every radio station is trying to exceed its own expectations/ RAJAR predictions, Radio Golha is, by intent and necessity, entirely limited in output. It has 200 hours of programming that it broadcasts in rotation. Those 200 hours are a mere fraction of 1500 hour-long programmes recorded over the course of 23 years, 1956-1979, for National Radio in Tehran. The 'Golha' ('Flowers Of Persian Song and Poetry') broadcasts comprised 1587 transmissions of Persian music and verse, ancient and modern, making use of a repertoire of over 250 classical and contemporary Persian poets, and innumerably more musicians, singers, orchestras. What you hear in the Golha is a combined effort of vision, preservation and innovation that changed the perception of musicians and poets in Iran (music was on the brink of illegality before the programme's success), and an encyclopaedia of traditional Persian music and ideas. Beyond that, you get goosebumps, an arched back, the starriest romance, the calmest voice, the most cosmic awe. Broadcast from an ex-pat Iranian site in the Netherlands, Radio Golha provides a tantalising snapshot of a touchstone in Persian culture, a touchstone in danger of disappearing off the map. I spoke to Jane Lewisohhn, a former SOAS student given a grant by the British Library to save the Golha archive from destruction. For her, the programmes are an untapped treasure trove imperilled by contemporary indifference in Iran.

"I've spent 20 years collecting tapes of the Golha broadcasts from private collectors in Iran and elsewhere and what always shocks me is how dangerously close to vanishing the Golha really were. Private collectors, who taped the shows when they were broadcast, die and their kids just junk them. I've still managed to retrieve 1500 hours of original broadcasts. It's been an urgent process. Which is odd considering the Golha programmes used to literally stop traffic. Every Thursday and Friday night for an hour Iran would grind to a halt so people could hear the Golha. It is a shared national memory that could've quite easily, in a physical sense, have simply disappeared. That would be a crime. Iranian music only started using notation in the Twenties. Before then this music was purely passed down 'chest to chest' as the Iranians say, heart to heart. Some of the music you hear in the Golha is truly ancient, older than ancient Greek music – of which none survives."

The 1979 revolution returned the Golha musicians to the same status they held before the Golha programmes started. By the 20th Century, musicians were denigrated as minstrels, had to use pseudonyms to avoid disgrace in everyday life, and developed as musicians under the private, reclusive tutelage of elder musicians who had carried the old songs for their whole lifetimes.

Jane: "Performance in public was unknown; this was a private, court music. At one such private party at the Italian

Ambassador's house in the early Fifties, Davoud Pirnia, the eventual producer of the Golha, hit upon the idea of mixing contemporary poetry with this music and modern orchestration, and actually bringing this music to the public. The first Golha programmes were extremely scholarly, intellectual and highbrow – pretty soon the producers realised the incorporation of modern poets and orchestras interpreting the ancient forms would be more interesting. We're talking about Fifties Iran here, a nation in which public music was banned, in which 85 percent of the population were entirely illiterate – so the Golha became something the whole nation enjoyed and made time for. It was a sudden supreme flowering of Persian culture."

So is the music and poetry you can hear in the Golha ancient or modern?

"Persian classical music, especially because it survived for so many thousands of years without notation, hasn't really progressed through key 'works' or key composers as such. It's a different notion of music than we have in the West. Here we think of music constantly developing new forms – in Persian music, as well as the Indian and Afghani classical traditions that grew from it, we have an alphabet of music that was laid down millennia ago, mainly by Sufi mystics, and then everyone who plays within that musical vocabulary is free to interpret it. So it's always an ancient music but it's always totally brand new and unique to the person playing within that tradition. Tradition isn't a creative straitjacket in Persian music; it's the building blocks from which you can make anything."

For over 30 years the Golha programmes explored that tradition, committing some of the most astonishing music you'll ever hear to tape. After a few hours in Golha's company even the snatches of Persian poetry start making total sense – the cadences and suggestions are unmistakable, and the way they occasionally blend with the full-blooded orchestral or solo piano renderings of old Iranian music makes what you're hearing blessed with both ancient glamour and post-war/ pre-revolution grit. These heart-stopping intros then give way to a longer musical performance within which you might get Sufi sitar, a solo ghazal, a Santur-backed torch singer or Khamenchi solo firestorm, or a nomadic love poet backed by the Golha-orchestra. Sometimes only God is meant to be listening.

Sometimes only a lover. All of it would be silenced by the '79 revolution.

Jane: "Because all of the music played on the Golha comes from the Sufi tradition of Islam, Khomeni was quick to stop the programmes, and pretty much outlaw all forms of musical expression for over a decade. When he finally relented to let musicians create again, he gave only 12 musicians in the entirety of Iran permission to play music – with strict curtailments that they couldn't play anything 'provocative'. Inevitably, the love poetry and songwriter tradition died a death – female singers, truly amazing voices who had contributed to the Golha's most incredible programming, were banned from performance, and still to this day women can't perform for mixed audiences in Iran."

Would you say that this music is now entirely forgotten in Iran?

"A very small group of musicians are still playing it, but with a disconnected emphasis on technique and abstract academia – that 'chest-to-chest' communication between elder and learner has gone. The memory is being erased. My final goal is to create an online database of the entire 1500 hours of programming, so people like you, like anyone, can explore this treasure trove. That's the dream – it's just sad that it takes people from outside of Iran to maintain this, because for Iranians the Golha are part of the national bloodstream, these songs are iconic to Persian culture. No one had bothered to make sure it wasn't lost forever."

If the Iranian revolution was prophetic, then the music contained in the Golha archive sadly isn't: I hear very little else from anywhere right now that quite matches its mysteries and magic, it's compassion and transcendence. Last word to Jane. Historical analysis aside – how does this music make you feel? "This music makes me travel. It takes me somewhere inexplicable, incredible – it links anyone with a heart to thoughts and longings as old as civilisation itself. It's basically one of the most deeply beautiful creations of the last century. It's up to the world to listen to it, learn from it and preserve it."

Contemporary culture has eliminated both the concept of the public and the figure of the intellectual. Former public spaces – both physical and cultural – are now either derelict or colonized by advertising. A cretinous anti-intellectualism presides, cheerled by expensively educated hacks in the pay of multinational corporations who reassure their bored readers that there is no need to rouse themselves from their interpassive stupor. The informal censorship internalized and propagated by the cultural workers of late capitalism generates a banal conformity that the propaganda chiefs of Stalinism could only ever have dreamt of imposing. Zer0 Books knows that another kind of discourse – intellectual without being academic, popular without being populist – is not only possible: it is already flourishing, in the regions beyond the striplit malls of so-called mass media and the neurotically bureaucratic halls of the academy. Zer0 is committed to the idea of publishing as a making public of the intellectual. It is convinced that in the unthinking, blandly consensual culture in which we live, critical and engaged theoretical reflection is more important than ever before.

9781846949555